# FIVE FACES of MINISTRY

**Pastor, Parson, Healer, Prophet, Pilgrim**

## Patricia Farris

Abingdon Press

*Nashville*

**Library of Congress Cataloging-in-Publication Data**

Farris, Patricia (Patricia Jean White)
 Five faces of ministry : pastor, parson, healer, prophet, pilgrim / Patricia Farris. — First [edition].
  pages cm
 ISBN 978-1-63088-688-2 (binding: soft back) 1. Pastoral theology. I. Title.
 BV4011.3.F374 2015
 253—dc23

2015014014

*To David, the unspoken presence on every page*

# Contents

Preface                                                vii
Introduction                                            ix

## Pastor

When It Happens                                          3
A Woman. Really?                                         5
Grounded in Integrity                                    8
Staying Steady                                          10
Learning to Collaborate                                 13
How Do You Do It?                                       15

## Parson

How Firm a Foundation                                   21
The Pastor's Study                                      23
The Fire-Breathing Deadline
    Monster (Preaching)                                 26
Ordering the Life of the Church                         29
The Buildings Witness                                   31
What Language Does God Speak?                           34
Reframing                                               37
More Than a Nonanxious Presence                         39

## Healer

Curate, Healer of Souls                                 45
Hospitality                                             48
Glimpsing a Whole World in Little Stories               51

"Clergy Health" Is More Than Metrics    54

Friends and Colleagues    57

The Blessing of Peaceful Sleep    60

Carrying the Anxious Weight of the
   Institutional Church    63

Sabbath Time    65

## Prophet

Stepping Up    69

The Newspaper and the Bible    71

Learning to Disagree (Deeply)    74

Seeing the Truth in One's Opponent    76

Pointing to Hope    79

Make Way for the Image of the Holy One    82

## Pilgrim

Where the Ministry Is Leading Us    87

With All Due Haste    89

An Elastic and Inquisitive Mind    92

Stability    94

Paying It Forward    96

Finding Funny    98

The Soundtrack    100

Postscript    102

# Preface

---

*Walk in love, as Christ also hath loved us.*

—Ephesians 5:2 (KJV)

---

**M**inistry in these times can be hugely perplexing. It can be frustrating and exhausting. It can wound, and it can heal. It requires deep roots and an agile gait. It is grounded in Benedictine stability and airborne on the wings of the Spirit.

Pilgrimage is the best metaphor I can conjure for the lived experience of the practice of ministry over time. As a pastor, I have mentored many who are walking the path. I have come to cherish this role of mentor and guide, teacher and companion, fellow traveler.

Among the fascinating developments in religious life in these early years of the twenty-first century is the renewed popularity of the pilgrimage to Santiago de Compostela in northeastern Spain. Each year, tens of thousands join in this ancient spiritual practice. Since the Middle Ages, Christians have walked one of the many routes across France and Spain to arrive at the Cathedral of Saint James in the grand plaza, joining thousands of others arriving daily for the Pilgrim's Mass. Some have started halfway around the world and have walked the complete route. Others have started at various points along the way or combined walking with bus and train interludes. Along the route, pilgrims are greeted by onlookers and fellow pilgrims with the traditional greeting: *"¡Buen camino!"*

There is no one way to do the pilgrimage. There is no timeline, no prescribed season. There is no language requirement, no age limit, no required credential. There is a network of routes etched into the earth by thousands and thousands of feet for over nineteen centuries. There is a company of travelers, fellow pilgrims, each wearing or carrying the scallop shell, numerous along the Galician coastline—the sign of baptism, the sign of Saint James. There is the shared journey, be it for adventure, for healing, for health, for insight, for testing, for encouragement, for wisdom, for love. And at the center, there is the heartbeat and breath of God.

I have never actually walked the route, but I have walked it in my heart and in my experience of ministry for over three decades. Wearing the symbolic scallop shell of our baptism, I have walked alongside new pastors as we ventured together into our calling, exploring the practice of ministry with honesty, vulnerability, repentance, celebration, expectation, sorrow, and hope.

I am deeply grateful to all fellow pilgrims—those who have gone on ahead, those who share the journey, and those just starting out or wondering if God might be calling them. To the congregations who have embraced me as pastor and fellow traveler, I owe humble appreciation and unending thanks. This is our story. And for the writing of this book, I offer special thanks to Sam Johnson for reading every word of the manuscript and making me a better writer.

As one who has been privileged to serve as guide and teacher, mentor, and fellow pilgrim, it is my prayer that this collection of reflections will encourage others still on The Way.

*¡Buen camino!*

Patricia Farris

# Introduction

Heaven knows we all need encouragement along the way. Keeping on in the practice of ministry in this day and age is no easy feat.

This collection of reflections on the practice of ministry is intended as a gift for those starting out on the journey and for those who've been at it awhile and more. It grows out of nearly forty years of doing ministry, trying to make sense of it, and all the while striving to learn more and be even more faithful each day, each week, each year. Along the way, I've also worked to give back as a clergy mentor to candidates and those just getting started. I've taught as an adjunct professor at the Claremont School of Theology, where I now serve as chair of the board of trustees. Having benefited immeasurably from those who took me under their wings or saw enough of a spark in me to invest time and prayer and expertise and opportunity into how I developed as a pastor, I am committed to giving back to those on the path.

Even at this point, I am always hungry for insights into how others do ministry. There's so much available about the "what" of ministry, but I always want to know about the "why" and the "how" and the "Who are you, really?" So while in many ways this is a book about how I go about the practice of ministry, my hope is that it will be a window that becomes a mirror and that together we might see more clearly the face of God and embrace more lovingly the yoke of Christ.

These reflections are grouped in five sections. "Pastor" examines questions of vocation. "Parson" gets at the nuts and bolts of doing the work. "Healer" muses on the things we do to bring health and wholeness and our own health and well-being as well. "Prophet" points to the hard work of engaging the injustice and brokenness of the world. "Pilgrim" sets our sights on the open road ahead, God's unfolding future of joy, promise, and hope.

You might read this book cover to cover. Or you should feel free to read the last reflection first or to pick it up and read whatever page presents itself. Or scan the contents and read what has a hint of helpfulness for you on any given day. This is a gift. It is yours to receive and enjoy in whatever way works best for you.

The quotations at the beginning and end of each reflection are designed to take you deeper—into the word of God or the hymnody of the church or the musings of a poet or sage whose insights provide color and feeling.

Several years ago when I was on a renewal leave, the Spirit led me right past my anticipated reading on the latest new approaches to ministry to the foundational work of Eugene Peterson, one of the best-known pastoral theologians of our time. In the process, I reclaimed this vocation and re-dedicated myself to the work that the church has entrusted me to do, work I believe God's people and God's world call me to do. I like the way Peterson crystallizes Jesus's invitation to us in *The Message*: "Walk with me and work with me—watch how I do it. Learn the unforced rhythms of grace" (Matt 11:28-30).

Let's walk and work together with one another and with Christ. It is a privilege. And more often than not, it is a joy and a huge amount of fun, moving together to the unforced rhythms of grace.

# Pastor

# When It Happens

*I will also put a new spirit in you to change your way of thinking. I will take out the heart of stone from your body and give you a tender, human heart.*

—Ezekiel 36:26 (ERV)

t happened during my first year of ministry in a local church. I felt in my bones what it means to be someone's pastor.

It was my first appointment to a local church. Our little congregation hadn't wanted a woman minister. They had made this quite clear to the district superintendent who had offered them the choice of a man nearing retirement, a man just out of seminary, or a woman coming from campus ministry on the East Coast. They picked in that order, but the bishop sent me. The move left my husband without a job. We didn't have kids, and we did have different last names. I didn't have much of a clue where to start, and they could see it in my eyes and hear it in my voice. The only way through that I could see was to work as hard as I could, even when I couldn't exactly understand why I was doing what I was doing.

Later the congregation and I joked that it took about nine months to really bring us together, a long gestation period that turned an episcopal appointment into a living relationship of pastor and people. Nine months peppered with trial and error, hurt feelings, missed cues, and earnest attempts. Nine months fueled by countless potluck suppers, coffee shared in diners, and someone's special pie. Nine months measured out in weddings, baptisms, funerals, sermons, worship, prayers, and long nights of wondering and second-guessing.

And then one day, everything shifted to a deeper level, the first inklings of love. It's the kind of love that doesn't make any sense except to those who are in it or have felt it, too. The kind of love that defies logic and takes us right to the heart of what conversion and salvation are really all about.

I saw it in Bob. He was a curmudgeonly old guy who scowled each week as he hurried out of worship. I cringed with each grudging handshake at the door. Then he had a heart attack, and I was at the hospital every day. Things happen in the hospital. Death sometimes visits there, but births and healing and new life are just as possible, too. Once Bob got through the worst part, I thought I detected a bit of a smile when I showed up, like just maybe he was actually glad to see me there at his side.

Some time later, he was back to a full and active schedule. One Sunday, he said something most unexpected at the door. He held my hand a bit longer than absolutely necessary and then, with an actual twinkle in his eye, announced: "Well, I've finally got you figured out . . . you're a communist!"

"What?!?" I asked. "Bob, whatever makes you think that?"

"Well, you're always talking about peace and love and things like that."

"Bob . . . you know, it's in the Bible!" I stammered.

"Yeah." He smiled fully now. "I knew you'd say that." And then he gave me a little hug.

Pastor is a relationship we live into with the people entrusted to our care. It's not a title that comes with an academic degree or an ordination certificate. It's not even a name we can give to ourselves, though we can learn to claim it and cherish it. And over time, we marvel frequently that fellow travelers would trust us enough to let us in at that deep, deep level of vulnerability and love. If it's true, it's of God, a pearl of great price that can only be bought with a pure heart and a generous spirit and as little ego attachment as is humanly possible.

---

*Take, O take me as I am;*
*summon out what I shall be;*
*set your seal upon my heart and live in me.*

—John Bell, "Take, O Take Me As I Am"

# A Woman. Really?

*In Christ's family there can be no division into Jew and non-Jew, slave and free, male and female. Among us you are all equal. That is, we are all in a common relationship with Jesus Christ.*

—Galatians 3:28 (*THE MESSAGE*)

One Sunday in the narthex before worship began, I was talking with one of our acolytes, a girl. I told her that when I was a girl growing up in church, we couldn't be acolytes. In school we couldn't be AV operators. She, of course, imagined that I was speaking of the Dark Ages. But that was in the 1950s. When I ventured off to seminary in 1974, I had never met an ordained woman. I had heard of *one*, but I had never actually seen her, let alone spoken with her.

I spent my first years in ordained ministry as a campus minister, preaching in a different church every Sunday. Whether in the pulpit or leading a discussion planned by United Methodist Women, the suggested topic was always the same: "Being a Woman in Ministry." Often I felt like the topic might as well have been "Being an Aardvark in Ministry" or "Being a Martian in Ministry." I knew I was normal, but so many seemed to find me strange or exotic.

Things didn't get easier right away when I transitioned into my first local church appointment. It wasn't always comfortable for me or for some in my congregation. Early on, there was a church member who didn't adapt particularly easily or graciously to my leadership. He complained about my voice. He counted how many times I'd say "brothers and sisters" or "sisters and brothers" and reported back to me weekly as if this were some sort of indictment or proof of transgression.

A sense of humor helped, along with a fairly secure sense of self and sense of call. I rehearsed the biblical stories, always careful to name the troublesome passages ("shall keep silence in the churches"; 1 Cor 14:34-35 KJV) as well as the liberating ones ("neither male nor female"; Gal 3:28-29

KJV). Then there were the great stories of Queen Esther, Judge Deborah, and Lydia and the reframing of Mary and Mary Magdalene. I rehearsed the historical stories about woman missionaries and John Wesley tapping women among his itinerant preachers. It was fun. But my favorite questions were usually the more personal ones: Could I get married? Wear makeup? And my all-time favorite: Could I wear earrings? After that, I always wore big earrings at church just because I could!

Despite as much progress as may have been made in the years since I started in ministry, many people still encounter me as the first ordained woman they have ever seen or heard. But then, maybe we haven't come so far. Last year a woman was named the first CEO of a major auto manufacturer in the United States. "A woman!" all the news reports exclaimed. Might as well have been a Martian.

I know enough about change to know that it comes hard and often cuts deep. It seems to hold all too true that the only one who really likes change is a wet baby. In fact, I can sometimes disarm people by confessing how much I myself hate change. Change one thing about baseball, and you'll hear about it from me! Instant replay on the baseball field? Hate it. Keep the human element, I say.

That's just it, isn't it? The human element. We humans cause the change, create the change, embody the change, resist the change, embrace the change, become the change. All in the image of God. I still remember the excitement I felt in a seminary class when, not having studied Hebrew, I learned that God's great "I Am" has no verb tense in Hebrew. Those two seemingly straightforward words can be translated in endless variations: I am who I was, I am who I am, I am who I am becoming, I was who I am becoming, I will be who I am becoming. And on and on.

At the very core of God is a cauldron of change, and as God sees it, it is all good. A number of years into our time together, my same contrary member launched a campaign to complete the stained glass windows in the sanctuary that had been put on hold for years due to initial budget limitations. Tracking down the original design for the window featuring John and Charles Wesley, he had it altered as a gift in my honor. He asked the artists to add in a depiction of John and Charles's mother, Susannah, who has been long credited with their deep faith and emphasis on scripture and social holiness.

It's always a mystery just how the heart opens. But it does. Claim your calling and stay the course! Anyone now excluded due to race or gender or language or sexual orientation will soon be right up front at the table, too. We will laugh and cry and wonder why it took so long. And we will give thanks to the One who has ever been and is ever becoming.

---

*She comes sailing on the wind, her wings flashing in the sun;*
*on a journey just begun, she flies on.*
*And in the passage of her flight, her song rings out through the night,*
*full of laughter, full of light, she flies on.*

—Gordon Light, "She Comes Sailing on the Wind"

# Grounded in Integrity

---

*And don't say anything you don't mean. This counsel is embedded deep in our traditions. You only make things worse when you lay down a smoke screen of pious talk, saying, "I'll pray for you," and never doing it, or saying, "God be with you," and not meaning it. You don't make your words true by embellishing them with religious lace. In making your speech sound more religious, it becomes less true. Just say "yes" and "no." When you manipulate words to get your own way, you go wrong.*

—Matthew 5:33-37 (*THE MESSAGE*)

---

et your *yes* mean yes and your *no* mean no," is how the Common English Bible translates Matthew 5:37. Scripture demands of us a kind of deep integrity in all that we say and do. This is a critical matter for all those of us who are "professional Christians." We become skilled at saying what we sense others would want us to say. We become glib with words and phrases that roll off our tongues easily, having uttered them so very many times. We can utter them whether or not they connect to our hearts any longer or in that moment. We can be totally distracted and still go through the motions, having rehearsed the part over and over again.

The gospel demands our *integrity*, a word that comes from the Latin, meaning "whole or intact." Integrity is the quality of being honest and trustworthy; the state of being whole and undivided; the condition of being unified or of sound construction. Being a person of integrity, a pastor of integrity, is a life's work. This sound construction is built day by day, word by word, action by action. This unity of self is nurtured in prayer and honest self-examination.

Our people watch. They want to know if we are the real deal. They want to know by observing us if this faith thing is really worth committing themselves to, as we have asked. Just a few weeks into a new pastorate, I was in the check-out line at the grocery store. A voice behind me observed, "Well, I see we're not cooking tonight!" I recognized my parishioner, though I could not yet recall her name. I wondered what the contents of my cart revealed to her about me. Did my choices speak to her of my values?

A colleague who studies these things reports that people in our communities pick up more of what we're about by how we live in our neighborhoods than by what we say in the pulpit. Our lives are our evangelism. These are folks who may never darken the door of our sanctuaries. Yet once they know we are the pastor, they take note. Do we care about our neighbors and inquire after their children and their aging parents? Do we look in on the one who has fallen ill? What's in our trash? Do we waste water? How do we spend our money? Do they see us smile or laugh? Are we someone they would like to know better? Do who we are and how we live communicate *good* news?

We all chafe at the idea of living in this fishbowl, our children especially so. Heaven knows we're not perfect, nor are we called to be so. But the stole we wear on Sunday, this symbol of the yoke of Christ, does not really come off when we leave the worship service. By our lives they will know us and will know the One who calls us and sends us and in whose service we are held.

A recent study shows that people checking out churches these days are looking for three things: the preaching, the worship and music, and above all, authenticity in the lives of the people there. Do we walk the talk? Are we for real? Does all this stuff we say we believe show up in how we live? Authenticity is the real key. We can put on the finest show, but if there's no "there" there, they will smell it and be gone quicker than we can say "hello."

Let your *yes* mean yes and your *no* mean no. In your words and in your deeds. And when we fall short, let us fall on our knees, confess, and pray that God teach us, heal us, and set us aright.

---

*Most merciful God, we confess that we have sinned against you*
*in thought, word, and deed,*
*by what we have done, and by what we have left undone.*
*We have not loved you with our whole heart;*
*we have not loved our neighbors as ourselves.*
*We are truly sorry and we humbly repent.*
*For the sake of your Son Jesus Christ, have mercy on us and forgive us; that we may*
*delight in your will, and walk in your ways, to the glory of your Name. Amen.*

*—Book of Common Prayer*

# Staying Steady

*They came to Capernaum. When [Jesus] was in the house, he asked them,*
*"What were you arguing about on the road?" But they kept quiet because on*
*the way they had argued about who was the greatest.*
*Sitting down, Jesus called the Twelve and said, "Anyone who wants to be first*
*must be the very last, and the servant of all."*

—Mark 9:33-35 (NIV)

It's another case of déjà vu all over again, as Yogi Berra might have observed. Disciples in Jesus's time as now have a confounding way of saying, talking about, and doing the most un-Christlike things. Somewhere along the road, the long road of discipleship, the old ways creep in and a kind of faith amnesia dims the light. We know better, but we revert. Thank heavens the evangelists saw fit to include stories like that in Mark 9 for us in the sacred text. We see ourselves in the bumbling and the stumbling of those Jesus himself hand-picked to follow him. Peter, Thomas, Judas, the ones who fall asleep in the garden—we are they. Disciples duck and betray. Disciples argue; they doubt; their egos get the best of them; their fears push aside their faith.

If part of the work of the pastor is to tend to the well-being of the flock and let not one wander off, how do we stay true? How do we keep awake? It helps to have the instincts and training of a good sheepdog—running about, nipping at their heels, herding them together and pointing them always in the right direction, all resting in the night by the still waters.

The analogy works as far as it goes, but parishioners are not sheep. They are intelligent. They talk back. Quite often their insights and ideas are much better than ours. They are working out their own salvation in the complexity of their own lives, families, and jobs, all of which are more central to their faith formation than the limited time they spend at church. Sometimes we remember to keep that in mind. We create a mental dashboard of relevant data in a focused and interactive way so as to keep the body moving on to perfection, as John Wesley puts it. But sometimes we forget, we slip, and we risk reacting in the moment when something hurtful is said or done. For the most part, Jesus exhibits a calm and thoughtful way of moving in these moments. "Come," he invites. "Let us sit down together. Let me not react to you but instead teach you something that you are actually on the verge of learning. See where your questions lead you. See how your fears inhibit your courage. See how your doubts open the door to deeper wisdom. Here—pull up a chair and join me at the table. Take, eat. Take, drink. Remember."

Across the years of ministry, I have come to understand this part of leadership as staying steady. I liken it to a kind of *basso continuo*, a continual base line in a musical accompaniment that sets the ground and stays steady as embellishments and harmonies form atop it. Sometimes it takes the form of a low drone, a note continually sounded through a piece. It is a baseline, a foundation, solid ground on which to stand, on which to walk. It is the steadying road.

It's fairly easy to see how this works in terms of pastoral work in times of illness and death. Very often our presence at a bedside or graveside is more about being than about saying or doing. A steadying manner is a way of embodying the psalmist's articulation of God's invitation to "be still, and know that I am God" (Ps 46:10).

Perhaps this practice of the discipline of staying steady finds its greatest challenge and greatest usefulness in times of change or of conflict. In a small congregation I served, decline seemed imminent. Yet ideas and opportunities were in abundance, all requiring change and new ways of doing almost everything. Meeting after meeting resulted in a firm and fearful no. Only a steady pastoral presence of love, assurance, and repeating the vision again and again began to create openings for the new life God was presenting.

There are moments when the change is too great or too slow or too frightening, and the pastor becomes the locus of resistance and anger. These are some of the worst times in ministry. Things are said and done out of hurt and anger that cut deep. It is so tempting to strike back or to walk away. Threats of "I may just have to leave this church" are heard.

"What were you discussing while you were walking on the road?" Jesus calmly asks. And then he proceeds to unpack it, sensing their fears and insecurity while holding them to a higher calling. In such times, there will be those who leave or fall away. But if we stay steady, never wavering in love, some will in time find a new way back in. Relationships will re-form on new ground. And the road will stretch out ahead of us, and we will walk on together.

---

*Peace I ask of thee, O River, peace, peace, peace.*
*When I learn to live serenely, cares will cease.*
*From the hills I gather courage, visions of the day to be.*
*Grace to lead and faith to follow. All are given unto me.*
*Peace I ask of thee, O River, peace, peace, peace.*

—Girl Scout songbook

# Learning to Collaborate

*God has put the body together, giving greater honor to the part with less honor so that there won't be division in the body and so the parts might have mutual concern for each other. If one part suffers, all the parts suffer with it; if one part gets the glory, all the parts celebrate with it. You are the body of Christ and parts of each other.*

—1 Corinthians 12:24b-27 (CEB)

My public grade school had a great music program. In the fourth grade, you could choose an instrument and play in the band or orchestra. I so wanted to play the trumpet. However, I got braces that year and the trumpet was ruled out. Instead, for some reason I don't exactly recall, I picked the viola. I don't know how I got from the brass section to the strings, but I thought a violin was too screechy and a cello too big to lug around. I played the viola all the way through college, even considering a professional career, until God and a call into ministry set me on another path.

Playing the viola taught me a great deal about the work of ministry. Part of it is the daily discipline of practicing. I can still remember the mornings I rolled over and turned off the alarm so as not to get up and have to practice before school. I can also remember my sore and blistered fingers in those early days. My parents remember the awful sounds I made so earnestly. I don't need to spell out the analogies to starting ministry to make the point.

But the real benefits to ministry were also unforeseen. As it turns out, violas most often play a supporting role in any ensemble. I fell in love with chamber music and string quartets, and that's where the real lessons for ministry came. A string quartet has no conductor. No one is in charge. Each of the four players is expected to come prepared and to carry their part. One learns to sense the timing and mood of the others. The quartet must move together and breathe together. Its success depends on all four players doing their utmost. There is no star. The beauty of its music comes when all four play as one.

This is my view of ministry, even as senior minister of a large church with an extensive staff. Each player is essential. Each must excel at what he or she does and prize his or her contribution. For ultimately, the beauty of the whole is not about one star. In fact, focus on a star takes away from the others and implies a hierarchy of importance that is antithetical to Jesus's model.

This runs counter to time-honored, lauded models of ministry. The "successful" churches of the 1950s and 1960s centered around a renowned preacher (man). The "successful" megachurches now also center around a charismatic, popular preacher (man). All I can say is that that's not how God has equipped me to do this work. I may play first violin nowadays, but I have total respect for the second violins, the violas, and the cellos of our team. I did have to learn, as a coach once pointed out, that I need to verbalize these expectations, as they are not necessarily understood or shared by those with whom I work. Not everyone played viola in a string quartet, though many have been on sports teams and can relate to the concept once I make explicit what my working assumptions are.

For me, there is no greater compliment than a staff person who says, "Thank you for confiding in me, for sharing with me, for taking time with me, for clearly valuing me." It breaks my heart to hear them say, "Most senior pastors aren't like that, you know." What? Why ever not?

I started out in ministry as a campus minister in Delaware. A real treat came in the fall when the geese would fly over in V formation. How I loved to see and hear them! And how delighted I was to later learn that they trade off being the lead goose. One leads the formation for awhile until tiring, then falls back, and another assumes the lead. In this way, their strength is multiplied. In a truly synergistic fashion, the whole is greater than the sum of the parts.

This, I believe, is Jesus's model for us. Each has a vital part to play: the boy with his loaves and fishes, the woman with the bucket at the well, Simon of Cyrene who carries the cross. Hail, supportive violas, one and all! May we make a new song, and may our music be sweet to God's ears.

---

*Sing GOD a brand-new song!*
*Earth and everyone in it, sing!*
*Sing to GOD—worship GOD!*

—Psalm 96:1-2 (*THE MESSAGE*)

# How Do You Do It?

---

*Keep thy heart with all diligence; for out of it are the issues of life. . . .*
*Let thine eyes look right on, and let thine eyelids look straight before thee.*
*Ponder the path of thy feet, and let all thy ways be established.*

—Proverbs 4:23, 25-26 (KJV)

---

**H**ow do you do it?" my friend asked quite sincerely. "Do what?" I
puzzled. "All of it—deaths, baptisms, weddings, funerals, hospi-
tals . . . How do you do it?" "Well, I just do," I fumbled, wondering to myself in that moment, *How* do *I do it?* I know very well that I am
not an unusually wise person or magnanimously compassionate. I often feel
at a total loss for words and second-guess what I have managed to utter. I
am an introvert in an extrovert's arena. When I think about it all too much,
I am certain that God and the church surely tapped the wrong person on
the shoulder. The British comedy ensemble Monty Python's *Life of Brian*
comes to mind. A young Jewish lad, Brian Cohen, born on the same day
and next door to Jesus, is mistaken for the Messiah. Outlandish situations
and dialogue follow as poor Brian tries again and again to slip out of this
mistaken identity and the expectations it carries.

Yet I *do* do it pretty much daily. I wade into situations and lives and
hearts and hurts and questions and joys beyond the telling. This is without
a doubt conclusive evidence, proof positive, of the veracity and power of the
grace of God and the limitless patience of the Holy Spirit. There are pastors
who relish this work. I am not one. There are pastors who come across as
being supremely confident of their abilities and gifts in these areas. I am not
one of those either. I am a rather shy person convinced that God is already
in the room before I get there and that mostly what I need to do is breathe
and look people in the eye and show them the face of Christ as best I can.

I have come to believe that in this regard, pastors are to become icon-
like. Since the fourth century, icons have been important to the Ortho-
dox churches of the Christian family. Painted in egg tempura on wood,

these tools for prayer and liturgy most often depict scenes of Christ, Mary, and the saints. Created by rules handed down from generation to generation, icons are venerated as representations of the divine, windows through which the soul can see the realities of the kingdom of heaven. Icons serve as a window inviting one's gaze to shift from the object in the foreground to the subject beyond. Their purpose, as Henri Nouwen has explained in *Behold the Beauty of the Lord: Praying with Icons*, is to pull one into the image in order to see through it and beyond it to the heart of God, to the reality of the great Mystery.

"Blessed are the pure in heart," Jesus said, "for they will see God" (Matt 5:8). Surely the seer and the seen must be of a pure heart or the vision will be blurred or obscured. There is no room for fakery or pretense here. There is space only for honesty and vulnerability, truth distilled to the essence of God's love, transparent and pure.

John Wesley said that God will bless the

> 'pure in heart' . . . with the clearest communications of his Spirit, the most intimate 'fellowship with the Father and with the Son.' He will cause his presence to go continually before them, and the light of his countenance to shine upon them. . . . They now see him . . . in all that surrounds them, in all that God has created and made. They see him in the height above, and in the depth beneath; they see him in filling all in all.
>
> The pure in heart shall see all things full of God. (Sermon 23, "Upon Our Lord's Sermon on the Mount," in *Sermons I*, § 6, ed. Albert C. Outler, vol. 1 of *The Bicentennial Edition of the Works of John Wesley* [Nashville: Abingdon, 1984])

The pastor's spiritual work is to draw as near to that place of pureheartedness as we are able, setting aside our ego, our fear, our arrogance, and our self-deprecation. God will fill the space within and between us with grace. And in those sacred moments when we most need to be present to others, God's light and love will emanate from our eyes, our words, our touch, our prayer.

The baby brought forward for baptism one Sunday was a precious little girl, a veritable miracle of God's grace and the advancements of modern medicine. Her parents stood proudly at the font. Her grandparents from two continents embodied the wide scope of God's love. The friends, colleagues, and gathered congregation radiated joy. She looked on calmly as I took her in my arms, dipped my hand into the life-giving water and baptized her, making the sign of the cross on her forehead. She smiled. Granted, these moments are not always so serene or beatific. But that day, as our tears mingled with the baptismal waters, the light of her smile lit the way to heaven.

*Change my heart, O God, make it ever true,*
*change my heart, O God, may I be like you.*
*You are the Potter, I am the clay.*
*Mold me and make me, this is what I pray.*
*Change my heart, O God, make it ever true.*
*Change my heart, O God, may I be like you.*

—Eddie Espinosa, "Change My Heart, O God"

# Parson

# How Firm a
# Foundation

*What you have received as heritage, take now as task
and thus you will make it your own.*

—Goethe

When I was a brand-new pastor, my bishop mentioned to me with some interest that he had read my recent column in our congregation's newsletter. A copy was mailed pro forma to the bishop's office, but I had no idea he or anyone else ever actually noticed, let alone took the time to read it. I was flabbergasted. I have no memory whatsoever of the topic, but what has stayed with me to this day is the fact that he took the time to check in on the well-being of one of his young pastors and that later, amidst the press of all the much, much weightier matters on his mind and schedule, he remembered it and remembered to say a word of encouragement to me.

A few years later, when I had grown into a position of leadership in our regional body, I ran into that same bishop at the annual meeting. He smiled when he saw me and asked: "Don't you love this?!" And my "Yes, I do!" came straight from my heart. We were kindred spirits who shared a love of the institution of the church. And even when he and I at times disagreed strongly about certain decisions, we did so out of mutual respect and the knowledge that we each yearned for the best possible decision that would undergird the whole and preserve its life long into the future.

I have a very strong sense of all the persons, lay and ordained, Methodist and other, who have mentored me in generous ways. While I believe that God gave me some basic raw material for the work of ministry, who I am today is thanks to this great company of dear colleagues who invested of their time, experience, love, and prayer in me, who encouraged me, who corrected me, who opened me to larger vistas for the church and for my own capacity.

I pay them back by the mentoring I now do with others coming along. But there's another piece to it as well. I believe in institutions, in the care and feeding of institutions. Institutions create the structures in which we serve and mentor. They are the body's skeleton. Institutions hold us together. They preserve and maintain our way of being, of serving.

In the days before I realized that God could call girls to ordained ministry, too, I envisioned a vocation of diplomacy or law. I majored in political science. I read de Tocqueville's *Democracy in America* and came to understand what it takes for a democratic form of government to exist, and sometimes to thrive. Through those studies, I learned that there's not much about all this that we ought to take for granted. A democracy and a representative form of government don't just happen. Some fundamentals are required—such as literacy, freedom of information, civil rights, accountability. I learned that our first president, George Washington, played a critical and proactive role in creating our precious republic and that he saw it as his aspirational duty to give it life, keep it alive, and equip it for a future.

Because of this formation, and because of the example of those who have mentored me and passed on to me a great, deep love of the church, I think institutionally. I choose to invest a lot of time into the institution that is the church at various levels. This does not mean that particular details of its current form are necessarily to be preserved at all costs. But it does mean that we who have benefitted by it and who know its benefits to the larger good have an obligation to care for it.

Some colleagues consider this work as a distraction from the "real" work of ministry that occurs in the life of the local congregation. I beg to differ. I have a sense of duty, of obligation. If our sense of the big time line of God's work in the world stretches both way back and way far into the future, something much more than the moment must be in place to hold all that together and carry it forward.

We are intergenerational, transgenerational stewards of something precious which ought never to be taken for granted. We honor the past and invest heavily in the future. And I am grateful that now, from a place in the great cloud of witnesses, my first bishop continues to hold me to it.

---

*Yet all these, though they were commended for their faith, did not receive what was promised, since God had provided something better so that they would not, apart from us, be made perfect.*

—Hebrews 11:39-40

# The Pastor's Study

*Thou shalt love the Lord thy God with all thy heart, and with all thy soul, and with all thy mind, and with all thy strength: this is the first commandment.*

—Mark 12:30 (KJV)

Having landed at an airport on the East Coast for a church meeting, I took a cab to my hotel. The driver, of indeterminate origin and with a heavy accent, said, "So, are you a politician?"

"Excuse me?"

"Are you a politician, A POLITICIAN?" By now I'm guessing he's Russian.

"No, I'm not."

"What are you?"

"I'm a pastor."

"Ooooh, a pastor . . . like a rabbi!"

"Right," I say. "Like a rabbi."

My rabbi friend and I had a great laugh about this later. A great deal of how we practice ministry is so similar. We've shared stories of congregational life, life in general, and vocation. We both do many of the same kinds of things—pastoral care, teaching, administration, worship leadership and preaching, congregational development. But there is at least one significant difference. The rabbi's office, like his home, is full of books. So are mine, but his congregation expects that he will take time, serious time, to read and study. His congregation even supports him in taking one month a year, free of other ministerial responsibilities, to study.

My love of reading and learning began with my mother taking me to the library or the bookmobile every two weeks. That was heaven, I thought, to check out the maximum number of books allowed, bring them back, browse the stacks, and head home with more. Every two weeks. All summer.

"Train children in the way they should go; / when they grow old, they won't depart from it" (Prov 22:6 CEB). Sure enough. Now I read pretty much constantly—articles, books, theology, fiction, two newspapers a day. I read online too, but really I prefer the old-fashioned way. Ink on paper. Something you can hold and feel and muse over and write on. Admittedly, it helps being married to a literature professor who has read more and more widely than I ever will.

Still, I feel constrained to read at home, out of sight, on my own time. If I'm "caught reading," it's as if I'm goofing off.

I've often wondered how the "pastor's study" became the "pastor's office." I remember an older colleague describing his schedule to me. Each day, he would take someone to breakfast to get to know them better, then read and study up through lunchtime, and then spend afternoons in the office or doing pastoral calls. When I've tried that, the staff is grumpy and resentful. Parishioners become suspicious. And the other work never seems to get done. So my office is my office and my studying takes place at home.

What happened? Is it American anti-intellectualism? Late capitalism? Postmodernism? The church's paranoid fixation on technique and growth schemes? Where did we stray from our vocation's center in the life of the mind as well as the life of the spirit, heart, and hands?

It's time to return to our roots and become more "like a rabbi" in this regard. I have created ways to build books into my ministry—a monthly congregational book study, writing book reviews for our denominational publication, quoting books in sermons in ways that elicit curiosity about the book or author, serving on the board of trustees of our regional seminary. Learning is like food to a rabbi and to a pastor. Without it we soon starve. Our preaching becomes repetitive and overly self-referential. Our world becomes too small.

I once said to a parishioner, himself a reader, that I thought heaven will be a place where we will have endless time to read all the books we ever hoped to read. He thought instead that once we're in heaven, we won't need to read because we will have all that knowledge and wisdom within. How I hope he's not right! For in God's perspective "a thousand years / are like yesterday past, / like a short period during the night watch" (Ps 90:4 CEB). And that's time enough for more books than I can even imagine.

John Wesley, himself interested in such disparate fields as medicine and electricity as well as theology, wrote, "It cannot be that the people should grow in grace unless they give themselves to reading. A reading people will always be a knowing people" (in a letter to George Holder on November 8, 1790).

I suggest we change the sign on our office door to "pastor's study" and close it from time to time. "Is she busy?" someone will surely ask. "Yes. She's reading." Now, and God willing, through all eternity.

---

*Open my eyes, that I may see glimpses of truth thou hast for me;*
*place in my hands the wonderful key that shall unclasp and set me free.*
*Silently now I wait for thee, ready, my God, thy will to see.*
*Open my eyes, illumine me, Spirit divine!*

—Clara H. Scott, "Open My Eyes, That I May See"

# The Fire-Breathing
# Deadline Monster
# (Preaching)

---

*Let the words of my mouth, and the meditation of my heart, be acceptable in thy sight, O LORD, my strength, and my redeemer.*

—Psalm 19:14 (KJV)

---

For more than thirty years now, most Sundays I'm in the pulpit, ready or not so much. I am a lectionary preacher, basing sermons on the three-year ecumenical cycle of scripture readings, and a manuscript preacher, carefully crafting a written sermon manuscript. Either of which makes me immediately suspect in the minds of many who claim to have certifiable proof that the demise of the church can be traced to these sorts of archaic hidebound practices. But after all these years, I know what I do well and I know what helps me do it; and God knows, in this endeavor we need all the help we can get.

This was revealed to me early on in my ministry. A friend had invited me to preach at her Sunday evening service. I don't remember the occasion or the text. I do remember the experience quite vividly. For some unknown reason, I had decided that this was an occasion to preach somewhat extemporaneously. Unchain myself from that manuscript, I imagined. Free at last to leave room for the Spirit to make an appearance. Driving to the church, I rehearsed my bare bones outlines repeatedly, excited and confident about this new venture.

My heart still freezes over when I recall stepping up—and yes, it was up—into that venerable old wooden pulpit. As I read the text and looked out over the congregation, my mind went blank. Wisps of the outline floated in and out but I could not hold them long enough to pursue a thought. Or so it seemed to me. I soldiered on through. I know that my mouth kept moving and I kept talking for the requisite amount of time out of sheer force of habit or will. Evidently, the Holy Spirit had been busy elsewhere that evening. I think that I was just way too far out of my comfort zone.

Early on in seminary, I staked my camp with those who argued that the discipline of the lectionary keeps us preachers from conveniently reverting to our favorite texts week after week. I still think that's true, although I admit that we are nevertheless tempted to revert to our favorite themes and become adept at pulling them out of almost whatever text presents itself. That temptation alone commends serious weekly study and an honest attempt to let the text first speak for itself.

I am also more attentive now to the texts which the lectionary omits. It was, after all, premised on the notion that the congregation was a fairly consistent company of folks who read their Bible at home daily, so that a few brief verses in Sunday morning worship were not the only Scripture they might encounter. We preachers are thus challenged to frame the larger story and even, from time to time, dare to take on what Phyllis Trible named the "texts of terror" in which women and children fare so badly. There's a whole big Bible out there, and we ought not to settle narrowly for the tried-and-true familiar passages.

I have my own internal criteria for how well I've treated the text. One is that different people each week comment on the sermon. I don't want the same four or five to tell me how brilliant I am, however gratifying that may be. Congregations are full of all kinds of folks at very different places in their faith journeys who learn in different modalities, who laugh at different illustrations, who are hungry for different forms of nourishment and challenge.

Another reaction I cherish comes when we have revisited a very familiar story and people say, "I never thought of it that way before. I never saw that in this story. I've seen myself—or God—in a new way today." That for me is confirmation that I have done my homework and am striving to keep the word fresh and alive for myself and my listeners as well. I'm not one who can pull out an old sermon and re-preach it. Never works for me. When I've tried that, I'm often embarrassed by something in it or see how poorly I'd expressed something or now see a whole new trajectory and meaning that had previously been hidden.

Admittedly, preaching is exhilarating and terrifying work. Some weeks, if I think about it too much, if I dwell on the sheer impossibility of communicating something worthy, something of God, to such a diverse and hungry company, I am nearly speechless. I think then of the words of a weekly columnist for the *Washington Post*, Kathleen Parker, who once described her muse as "the fire-breathing deadline monster." Cautioned by my doubt, I must not tarry there. Sunday will come. And if we've faithfully spent time in prayer and study and pastoral care and reflection on the world, and if our hearts are open and our intent sincere, the Holy Spirit always shows up.

---

*Lord, to the end that my heart may think, that my pen may write, and that my mouth may set forth Thy praise, pour forth into my heart and pen and mouth Thy grace.*

—Bernard of Cluny

# Ordering the Life of the Church

---

*Just think—you don't need a thing, you've got it all! All God's gifts are right in front of you as you wait expectantly for our Master Jesus to arrive on the scene for the Finale. And not only that, but God himself is right alongside to keep you steady and on track until things are all wrapped up by Jesus. God, who got you started in this spiritual adventure, shares with us the life of his Son . . . He will never give up on you. Never forget that.*

—1 Corinthians 1:7-9 (*THE MESSAGE*)

---

With ordination comes authority for the ministry of Word, Sacrament, Order, and Service. Quite frankly, at the time of my ordination, I had little idea of what the work of "ordering the ministry of the church" would entail. Sure, I had grown up nurtured in the life of a wonderful congregation. I was aware of committees. My accountant dad was on the church finance committee longer than any one person should have to endure. But still, to my eyes, everything just seemed to run by itself. I had little notion of the work of knowing the congregation's gifts, recruiting and nurturing volunteers, training people in how to conduct meetings and bring forth the wisdom and creativity of the group, or guiding the whole while tending to all the parts.

As a result, I learned a lot the hard way. Lots of trial and even more error. Most every pastor is blessed by a few lay people who see through us and step up to make sure we don't crash and burn. But in the long run, it's up to us to embrace this part of our responsibility and learn how to do it well. It's about building up the body so that individuals may grow and the ministries and mission of the congregation can be as effective and faithful as we can support them to be.

Years ago I was pastoring a small church with tired, aging members whose energy had long-since ebbed. Even when sparked by a vision, they found it hard to muster the courage to take it on. Worse, I, too, was focusing on what we were not able to do, the resources we didn't have, the obstacles to just about everything anyone thought of.

A Catholic sister leading a "church revitalization" workshop I attended out of desperation shocked me back to life by saying, "You have all the gifts you need. God has already given you everything you need." My first reaction was denial. You don't know us, Sister. That might apply to every other church in this room, but not mine! Our group discussion quickly proved me wrong. We all needed to cut the self-pity, do a one-eighty, and reframe the possibilities and gifts the Holy Spirit was indeed offering.

This seems to be a lesson that I need to relearn over and over. Negativity has an ugly way of seeping back in. Years later, in a large church with seemingly endless resources, I was scrambling to find someone to chair a key committee. "Ask Bill," a member kept urging. Not wanting to admit that I didn't know the first thing about Bill, it took me a couple years to check him out. Perfect: professional expertise, measured temper, sense of humor, project-oriented, love of the church. The mission and ministries of the church thrived with his leadership.

There are times, of course, especially as the annual meeting of the congregation looms, when it's tempting to reduce "ordering the life of the church" to filling slots and compiling reports. This is the "rearranging the chairs on the deck of the Titanic" sinkhole. Instead—resist the centripetal pull. Hold on and aim high. Pray to gain insight into where and in whose life the Spirit is working at this moment and invite that person into deeper discipleship and new leadership opportunities. Call forth their gifts, then support and nurture them in living into them. Build up the parts so that the whole body can thrive. Keep the focus on gifts, timeliness, and the mission of the church. Maintain a balance between internal church needs and outward-reaching community needs.

The work of ordering the life of the church is really the work of an artist—a sculptor, painter, kite-maker, musician, poet. It's about looking unflinchingly at what is and seeing and hearing and imagining so much more. It's about shaping the raw materials and securing the infrastructure so that the church can be "the church in the power of the Holy Spirit" as Moltmann put it. Help it fly. Hear it sing. Watch it grow. See it serve.

---

*Spirit of the living God, fall afresh on us.*
*Spirit of the living God, fall afresh on us.*
*Melt us, mold us; fill us, use us.*
*Spirit of the living God, fall afresh on us.*

—Daniel Iverson, "Spirit of the Living God" (slightly reworked)

# The Buildings
# Witness

*Lord, You have been our dwelling place in all generations.*

—Psalm 90:1 (NKJV)

Photographs from the early 1950s show the construction of our current sanctuary. The steeple rises to over 120 feet and towers over the newly planted trees along the street. The trees are much taller now, but the steeple is still a distinguishing feature on our skyline. It was built in a time of some hubris on the part of the church, to be sure, so confident the steeple was of its prominence, vitality, and bright future. Times have changed. The church's role in the life of the community has shifted, mediated by an ever-changing religious landscape, a radically altered economy, and an increasingly more diverse population.

Even so, that steeple still speaks. Our many visitors report being drawn to the church in one of two ways—by viewing the website or by literally seeing the steeple. Recently, a neighbor came to request a memorial service for her husband who had just died. She knew nothing about us except for that steeple and the buildings and grounds. We seemed welcoming, she said, and enduring. That steeple had been there through all their years of living nearby, and in her time of need it beckoned to her just as if there were a big "GOD LOVES YOU" sign on top.

Buildings speak. After years of benign neglect, we did some modest relandscaping across the front of the church and at the parsonage. Neighbors stopped to talk and comment on the improvements. A sense of energy and excitement enlivened conversations as if the very newness of it all communicated a word of hope. Much more than we had realized, this work signaled our investment in the community, our commitment to stay. It spoke of a love of God, a love of nature, a love of neighbor more than a marketing campaign could ever hope to do. Bricks and plants and flowers and paint all singing an ode to joy. The people walking by stopped for a while. They stopped in. It was like a big party that no one had intentionally planned.

There is a critique of church buildings swirling about at the moment. Buildings, without a doubt, can weigh the church down and drain its ever-limited coffers of funds much needed for ministries and mission. Buildings can also become idols, prisons of a once-glorious past. Buildings can become ends in and of themselves. And of course run-down church buildings can house vibrant ministries so wonderful that no one notices the peeling paint and the sagging door frames. Moreover, the critics maintain, real ministry happens outside those walls in the lives of people and communities.

True enough to all of that. And yet. Buildings witness. Buildings speak. They can speak of welcome and hospitality. They can be open to the community in ways that bring people together for discussion, art, music, study, twelve-step groups, and plain old-fashioned fun. They create common space, what sociologists call "bridging social capital," that is, building cooperative connections between people from different walks of life, fostering social inclusion. They nurture community, and communities, in a time when so much conspires to unravel the very things that draw us together and reinforce the common good. They can be both confessional and communal, blurring the boundaries between insiders and outsiders, us and them. And this is a great gift.

Adjacent to our big sanctuary with that very tall steeple stands a small chapel. We open the front door daily. The sign out front reads: "Chapel Open for Prayer." People stop in, frequently leaving written prayer requests on the prayer board in the narthex. Often people leave notes or mail them to the church with a few dollars to help with costs. "Thank you," people have said. "I pass your church every day on my way to work and even though I don't have time to stop and come in, your sign and that open door remind me to pray." Another wrote, "Walking by the church makes me feel better. It gives me peace."

Buildings witness. We are their stewards—not solely for the internal purposes of the church itself, but for all the ways our very buildings proclaim a message of God's inclusive, welcoming, sheltering, abiding, and community-creating love.

---

*This is the house of God. This is the gate of heaven.*
*This is a holy place. You are always welcome.*
*Trust and know that I'm always with you,*
*through all changes and all seasons, when you wake and when you're sleeping.*
*All is well. All is well.*

—Mariénne Kreitlow, "This Is the House of God"

# What Language Does God Speak?

*What language shall I borrow*
*to thank thee, dearest friend?*

—"O Sacred Head Now Wounded"

t is our congregation's tradition to put up a big manger scene each year outside in the central courtyard. From my second-floor office window, I regularly witness little Christmas miracles down at the manger, miracles that bring great joy. One Advent, the church's former asphalt parking lot across the street was being transformed into a new transitional shelter for homeless families, which included underground parking for the church as well. Day after day, the mostly Spanish-speaking laborers would cross the street at some point to pay homage to the Baby Jesus, Mary, and Joseph. They prayed in Spanish. I know the Holy Family heard and comprehended their every faithful word.

We host a Swedish school that meets at the church weekly. I had no idea that there were so many Swedes in the Los Angeles area until this group came to us. They are young parents who want to pass on their culture and language to their children who are growing up here in the States.

One December, late in the afternoon as the sun was going down, I was walking past the crèche. I saw a little girl standing right by the manger. She had climbed inside to get close to the Baby Jesus, and she was just tall enough to look over the edge. She was leaning in close to his face and talking. And as I drew near, I could hear that she was speaking to the Baby Jesus in Swedish. He must surely have been responding to her, because she was carrying on quite something of a conversation with him. Her dad stood patiently nearby, wisely knowing the importance of such a precious moment in the life and faith of his little daughter. I thought it wonderful to know that Jesus speaks fluent Swedish. And that even as a newborn Babe, he could converse with a little girl because she believed that he could and would.

I may be more open to accepting such things because of the year I spent living as an exchange student in the south of France with a French-Mediterranean Catholic family. There, of course, God spoke French, and some Italian, if truth be told. In those heady days not long after Vatican II, the whole Catholic Church seemed to be discovering that God in fact speaks all the languages of God's human children, in addition to the Latin long ascribed to God officially by the Church. Mass in the vernacular was a really big deal.

I live now in a metropolitan area where the latest statistics show that more than 54 percent of the people speak a language other than English at home and in their private lives—not only Spanish but also Korean, Vietnamese, Armenian, Cambodian, Persian, Swedish, and dozens of other languages, more than ninety-three languages among our children in the Los Angeles Unified School District.

The founders of Methodism, the brothers John and Charles Wesley, apparently got it. Our calling, as Charles Wesley put it in one of his many hymns, is to "serve the present age" in all its splendor and multiplicity ("A Charge to Keep I Have," in *The United Methodist Hymnal* [Nashville: The United Publishing House, 1989], 413). John set a fine example. He took language study seriously, learning German in order to translate hymns. And when he came to the Colonies to grown in faith, serving for a time in Georgia, he quickly found that he couldn't communicate with the diversity of the parishioners he found. He took it upon himself to also study Spanish, Italian, and even French, although to my regret he didn't think much of it, calling it "the poorest, meanest language in Europe; that it is no more comparable to the German or Spanish than a bagpipe is to an organ" (October 11, 1756, *Journals and Diaries IV (1755–1765)*, ed. W. Reginald Ward and Richard P. Heitzenrater, vol. 21 of *The Bicentennial Edition of the Works of John Wesley* [Nashville: Abingdon, 1992]).

I'll leave it to others to debate the merits of learning Hebrew and Greek for serious, in-depth scripture study. But I will take a strong stand with those who argue that pastors should be at least bilingual. Learning another language does so much more than make it possible to converse with others, as critical as that is. A language is a window into another's way of seeing the world. Language study engenders humility while it opens onto new realms of beauty and expression.

And if indeed each and every one is created in the image of God, what riches have we yet to explore of the manifold ways God speaks all the languages of the human mind and heart, hears us all, understands us all, comforts and receives us all, honors and cherishes us all?

---

*Come, sinners, to the gospel feast; let every soul be Jesus' guest. Ye need not one be left behind, for God hath bid all humankind.*

—Charles Wesley

# Reframing

**M**y friend lay strapped down to a gurney in the ER. Having fainted and fallen face forward, his head, neck, back, and legs had been secured by the paramedics until everything could be checked out. After a few minutes of waiting for the doctor, minutes that seemed like hours, he was getting antsy and a bit claustrophobic. "Please see if they can let me loose," he pleaded. I checked. Nothing doing—too risky. "Bill," I said, "you're just going to have to reframe this. Relax and take some deep breaths." We began breathing together as we waited.

This story has a happy ending. The only damage done amounted to a few cuts and bruises. We have laughed and laughed about my directive to him to reframe. At the time, I wasn't sure where that came from as I heard the words come out of my mouth. Later I realized that it's at the heart of much we do in ministry.

Reframing is more than spinning, which has negative connotations of evasion and deception. Reframing is about seeing through to a different reality. It is a new way of seeing and apprehending. When people move away from our congregation, it's often accompanied by a deep sense of sadness and loss. At the same time, I realized some time ago, that very sadness is a clear indication of the depth of love shared. If it were easy to leave, or worse, if someone couldn't wait to get away or if everyone was breathing a sigh of relief at their departure, that would be a sign of something much worse. It's the love that hurts and causes the pain. That's sadness reframed as an expression of love.

One of the hardest parts of being a constantly changing congregation is what the congregants see and feel in Sunday worship. It's literally the glass half empty/full dichotomy. Longtime members see empty spaces in the pews, the shadow of friends and loved ones no longer present. Ask them about new, younger visitors, and they say "Who? I didn't notice them."

They literally don't see the people they don't yet know or the people who don't look like the people who used to be there. Newcomers see a vital congregation made up of people gladly serving Christ and growing in faith. They see children and youth and seniors and families and singles.

The pastor sees both, feels both the loss and the vitality. It's a choice to stay in half-full mode, or better yet, to reframe half-full as full of something new that can't quite yet be fully articulated. "I am creating something new. / There it is! Do you see it?" says the Lord (Isa 43:19 CEV). Our job is to see, and then to name it in such a way that it reframes the *what is* for others to see as well.

Same goes for the world as well. I have been on several mission trips to Africa—Madagascar, Zimbabwe, Mozambique. Much of life there breaks the heart. The challenges can feel hopeless or simply totally overwhelming. And yet . . . and yet there is a spirit, a strength, a beauty, a potential that is palpable. It is our job as pastors to name that and to reframe the perceptions so relentlessly repeated in the media, all those images of disease and poverty and violence and hunger and despair, images that lead to disengagement and global neglect.

A wonderful book entitled *The Bright Continent* reframes our commonplace sense of "the dark continent" to see its potential and ingenuity. Journalist Dayo Olopade argues for seeing Africa through African eyes rather than through Western frames. Lean economics, she says, are an invitation to innovate. And what she sees are incredible tenacity, ingenuity, perseverance, and creativity.

The world finds ways to write off the needs and the potential of the poor, of anyone who is "other." We need to reframe. These are our brothers and sisters. Rabbi Jonathan Sacks quotes an old Jewish teaching that says that God makes every person in the same image—God's image—and each is different. Each is a child of God.

God is always bringing forth new life. God is making the church new, too. It won't look like the way church used to look. Our spiritual work is to reframe, to believe and to trust and to see our way together into the new thing that our God is doing.

---

*Do not be conformed to this world, but be transformed by the renewing of your minds, so that you may discern what is the will of God—what is good and acceptable and perfect.*

—Romans 12:2

# More Than a Nonanxious Presence

*Christian hope opens us . . . to the gift of the future promised by God.*

—Gustavo Gutiérrez

Coming to my first local church appointment in California from the East Coast, about the only thing I had been told about the place was that it was "a beautiful plant." Indeed, the sanctuary was quite lovely. What the district superintendent had failed to mention included such details as the discovery about a month prior of the body of a young Vietnamese refugee in the dumpster in the parking lot or the arsonist who was systematically setting fire to places of worship throughout town. As the truism goes, seminary had not prepared me for this.

Perhaps these early experiences in ministry were setting the stage for much of what would come. The newsworthy crises included a major earthquake and a city torn apart by racial injustice. The ecclesial crises when later I myself become a superintendent included clergy sexual abuse, child abuse, embezzlement, and several lawsuits.

At one point, when facing a major challenge to my leadership, I hungrily read all the available books on leadership. The notion of being a "nonanxious presence" was prevalent at the time. It has to do with staying calm, not being reactive, defusing the anxiety of the situation by being centered and steady.

That image spoke to me in profound ways and gave me words for some of what I had instinctively known to do. Maybe it's because I'm something of a still-waters-run-deep kind of person by nature. My response to almost every challenge is to withdraw into silence for long periods of reflection and plain old mulling-over. Maybe I was a desert tortoise in an earlier life. In those times of silence, whether I'm sitting or walking, the clearest way God speaks to me is by sending verses of hymns into my awareness. When I'm paying attention, those words offer just what I need to make it through. Once, when I was feeling beleaguered, "His Eye Is on the Sparrow" just started playing in my head, and the tears flowed, and I knew God's presence would carry me through. It's my way of staying rooted in prayer.

But I've also learned that being a nonanxious presence is not enough. It is foundational, but not enough. It's important to engage the crisis, to unpack it and discover how it needs to be engaged, and in some cases, managed. Leadership is needed to fashion not only a response but also a way forward. It's about naming hope and making it visible.

Often that means taking action. In those early years, I quickly learned that a neighbor congregation housed the offices of the refugee resettlement organization. We reached out to them and initiated a series of community meetings to build closer relationships with the newcomers in our midst. We also banded together with several congregations to hire a security firm. We all breathed a huge sigh of relief when the arsonist was arrested and later convicted, though to this day I am convinced that a mental institution would have been more appropriate than jail for that lost soul who could not abide the thought of graven images in a house of worship.

Later I learned how to frame a situation, how to put words on it that could make it somehow manageable, or at least bearable. I learned how to work with the press to put public words on how a story might be reported. And I learned how to take a situation back, how to reframe it when necessary, to tone it down, or diminish its negative impact.

Now, when crises arrive in my congregation, as they will, I know to treat them seriously but am not usually undone by them. It takes internal work and requires a kind of learning that we should not expect seminary to impart. It's on-the-job training.

Jesus shows us all these modes of leadership. He draws apart for prayer. He calms the wind and the waves. He recounts words of the prophets and the psalmists to ground and to guide. And through it all, he keeps moving forward. He shows his followers how to keep moving forward as well. He is not fear-less. He sees and feels and senses and knows too much for that. He keeps them all moving forward anyway. These things going on around you, he'd say, here's what they mean. Here's what God is doing. Here's the good news. Here's where hope is to be found.

*Hope-full are those who long for better days,*
*for they have arrived in a place where God dwells.*
*Hope-full are those who companion the distressed, for they shall not be overwhelmed.*
*Hope-full are those who bring the anxious to rest, for theirs is a crucial role.*

—Bruce Thompson, "The Hope-fullness of Life"

# Healer

# Curate, Healer
# of Souls

An old-fashioned word for pastor is *curate*, a healer of souls. One would think this would be a foundational, formative identity. But it is quickly passed over or set aside or simply forgotten in the daily stress and busyness of things to do, programs to lead, and budgets to make. I've never been asked in an annual evaluation, "Did you cure souls of the precious people of this community this year?" The word *curate* calls us back, calls us deep, to the vocation Jesus invites us into in the first place—to fish for people, to touch their souls with love and grace and healing beyond their imagining.

You'd think we would learn. After all, it's more the norm than the exception that one's carefully planned out week is disrupted by the pain and messiness of life—the call to come to the bedside of one nearing the end of earthly life, the rush to the hospital to weep with the young parents of a stillborn child, the unscheduled visit of one still reeling from the invitation into forgiveness from last week's sermon.

You'd think we'd know. Granted, Jesus lived long before the days of cleverly crafted digital devices to assist in the plotting and parsing and documenting of the use of time. Still, none of the Gospels reveal his daily or weekly planned agenda: Tuesday, 17th week. Breakfast with key leader.

Strategy session with disciples. New sandals. Public community forum. Conflict intervention session with disciples. Dinner with Mom.

Apparently for the evangelists, the really important things were what happened along the way, regardless of Jesus's plans—the woman touching his garment, the friend whose brother has just died, the crowds who press him to continue long past the stated hour of adjournment, the story he calls to mind and needs to tell, the bread to be broken and shared, some moments apart to rest and pray.

We are curates as we move among our people. The story of the life of Jesus shows us again and again that ministry is about paying attention in the moment. It is about noticing the openings for conversation, the ache for acknowledgment and validation. Sometimes it is about finding those few needful words. Sometimes it is about naming the gifts—forgiveness, grace, promise, assurance, peace, hope. Sometimes it is about receiving the tears and anger. And sometimes it is about being willing to sit in silence for as long as it takes.

We are curates as we preach. Very often I am reminded that if healing comes, it is through the gift of Christ working in and through us rather than something we had planned or intended. "It is Christ who lives in me," Paul wrote to the Galatians (2:20). A man came to me some weeks after a sermon I had preached. I hadn't particularly remembered it, having raced on to the work and activities of the subsequent weeks. When he quoted parts of it back to me over coffee, it didn't even sound much like anything I would have actually said, or at least not how I would have said it. But what he heard in his heart had changed his life. He had travelled across country to sit at his mother's graveside, where he wept, was able to forgive her for painful parts of his childhood, and lay down the anger and resentment he had carried forward until that day.

Usually healing is not so dramatic or even obvious. Healing happens at the Blessing of the Animals when a cherished pet is remembered. Healing happens when one struggling with addiction finds courage to go another day. Healing happens when old animosities are set aside. Healing happens when one hears that who one is, is enough. Healing happens when a frightened child lights up at hearing her name.

We are curates as we administer the sacraments. As the children came forward to receive communion one Sunday, one new little girl looked at the plate of bread, prepared in small pieces to be dipped into the cup. She looked me in the eye and asked, "Can I take more than one? I really need it this week!" She moved on gripping a handful of bread. The outward and visible sign of an inward and spiritual grace. Healing. And strength for the journey.

---

*Fill my cup, Lord;*
*I lift it up, Lord;*
*Come and quench this thirsting of my soul.*
*Bread of heaven, feed me till I want no more.*
*Fill my cup, fill it up and make me whole.*

—Richard Blanchard, "Fill My Cup, Lord"

# Hospitality

---

*Oh yes, my house of worship*
*will be known as a house of prayer for all people.*

—Isaiah 56:7b (*THE MESSAGE*)

---

For a season in the life of our congregation, we focused on the practice of hospitality. Long a large, prominent, self-sufficient church, we wanted to turn our gaze outward, to open not only the doors but the life of our congregation. We studied Christian hospitality. We prayed; we did role plays. We examined our signage and trained our ushers and greeters. We switched to better, fair-trade coffee. We gussied up our restrooms and expanded our ministries for children and families. We listened to the stories of those who showed up and invited them to a meal together. And we opened every worship service singing "All Are Welcome."

That last bit was my idea. Even the music director didn't much like it, but I persevered. One day, after months and months of singing "all are welcome in this place," one of our congregational leaders said, "You know, we keep singing that song. Maybe we'd better act like we really mean it." By then, we had lumbered far on down the road toward genuine hospitality, and we were ready to recognize that we still had a long way to go to make it much more than a new set of behaviors. We sought to claim hospitality as a mark of our fundamental identity.

Some changes were subtle. Some were jarring. Some were both. Like most churches, the location of our restrooms was a well-kept secret. "They're right over there," old-timers would say, as if it were self-evident. We had to step back and try to see everything through the eyes of a first-timer. Kitchen? Coffee? Nursery? Church office? Oh, how many times did we instruct people to do this, that, and the other thing in the church office, before it dawned on us that only a handful of folks knew where it was and how to get there? Might as well have been the Holy Grail.

At the beginning, we found it hard to agree on just what communicated what we intended. As more and more visitors and newcomers showed up, we started printing the words to the Lord's Prayer in the Sunday bulletin. We reasoned that if new folks didn't know the words, they would not only be excluded from prayer, they'd be made to feel like outsiders. "What are we doing now?" some complained. "We're wasting space and paper. Everyone knows this."

But what if they don't? It goes for most everything. All the stuff in the sanctuary. The nativity scene. The pledge drive. The inside jokes. It's all a foreign language if you haven't grown up with it. And if it's true that a huge percentage of young adults have never been inside a church for any reason, as they say, not even for a wedding or funeral, what in the world do they make of our secret codes and rituals?

We moved the coffee to right outside the front door. We put up signs. We try hard now to pay attention and to decode what we do and say. Never assume. Ask questions. Put yourself in their shoes. It's hard to realize that for many folks, going to church is like travelling to a foreign country where the language and customs seem intentionally designed to cause confusion and disorientation. Some folks relish that feeling. Most do not.

Sometimes, hospitality just means getting out of the way. Not talking so much. Letting the sacred space offer its own invitation. Showing it in its best light, free of clutter, liberated from usefulness. Trusting that God wants to connect, and people want to connect, and our main job is to avoid being in the way.

I knew we'd made some progress when a newcomer explained why she started coming to this church: "I saw many people engaged in trying to live Christlike lives. Their smiles and open-mindedness were a balm to my loneliness." As Buck Owens sings it, "No more loneliness, only happiness, love's gonna live here again."

Hospitality is not so much about technique or best practices, though those things are important. It's so much more about open hearts and open minds. It's about an integrity of discipleship that shows. And that makes space for the Holy Spirit to walk right in and stir up all kinds of stuff. Once you start down this path, there's no end to the adventures that await. There are no finish lines, only wider circles of love ahead.

*Let us build a house where love can dwell*
*And all can safely live,*
*A place where saints and children tell how hearts learn to forgive.*
*Built of hopes and dreams and visions,*
*Rock of faith and vault of grace;*
*Here the love of Christ shall end divisions;*
*All are welcome, all are welcome,*
*All are welcome in this place.*

—Marty Haugen, "All Are Welcome"

# Glimpsing a Whole World in Little Stories

---

*For just as the body is one and has many members, and all the members of the body, though many, are one body, so it is with Christ. . . . Indeed, the body does not consist of one member but of many. If the foot would say, "Because I am not a hand, I do not belong to the body," that would not make it any less a part of the body. And if the ear would say, "Because I am not an eye, I do not belong to the body," that would not make it any less a part of the body. If the whole body were an eye, where would the hearing be? If the whole body were hearing, where would the sense of smell be?*

—1 Corinthians 12:12, 14-17

---

A couple years ago, a homeless man started showing up at our church regularly. He was very quiet. He bothered no one and declined offers of food with a mere shake of his head. The only point of communication was in his eyes, so it seemed. Some days they seemed vacant. Some days we connected. Some days he looked hurt or angry as if to say that it had been a bad night or a hard time on the street.

Gradually, he became part of the church community. From the periphery, he moved tentatively toward the outer edges, showing up at coffee fellowship briefly, then moving back. He'd be around on Sunday mornings but never come inside the sanctuary. The liturgical dance of the early church, the Tripudium, was two steps forward, one step back. With William we gradually began to dance, tentatively, cautiously. We missed him on Sundays when he was a no-show. Something felt wrong.

Over time, months and months actually, he started showing up in various small groups as well. I observed his progress from the back of a room where he sat alone, to a table with others where he neither spoke nor ate, to occasions when he would raise his hand as if to speak, as others did, until called upon, when he would demur. The dance continued.

He showed up more often and earlier for worship. He'd come inside and sit in the very back pew closest to the exit. Gradually he moved closer to the front. One Sunday, I noticed him participating in the passing of the peace. By this time, the congregation had embraced him, too. If visitors looked at all hesitant or fearful of his appearance, I'd hear people simply say, "Oh, that's William. He's part of our congregation." This, mind you, in a place where twenty years ago ushers wore suits and nothing untoward would have been permitted.

William's presence in our midst has taught me a lot about the body of Christ. At first, I assumed he was there, as many are, for food or money, or other things hard to come by on the street. He came instead for fellowship and human contact. He has never asked for anything. William came for God's love and ours.

One Sunday I was flying around in pre-worship hectic mode. A parishioner reached out for a hug and hearty hello. William, standing nearby, said, "Me, too" and gave me a huge bear hug. It was the first time we'd touched. Later the image of doubting Thomas needing to touch Jesus's wounds came into my reflections on the day. This is incarnation, the Word made flesh. Love heals our brokenness and makes us whole.

The next time we received persons into membership, we invited William to become a member. He didn't actually say yes but he listened. He didn't show up on the Sunday we set aside for reception of members. The next week, we gave him the membership certificate I'd signed with his name in beautiful calligraphy on the envelope. Later in the service, he came forward for communion for the first time. He knelt and bowed his head. "This is my body broken for you; this the cup of salvation."

In the liturgy of the sacrament of Holy Communion, "This Holy Mystery" as United Methodists call it, after all have communed, we pray together, "By your Spirit make us one with Christ, one with each other, and one in ministry to all the world." There is so much about William we still do not know—his full name, where he stays during the week, how he came to live on the street, whether he has family somewhere worried about him. Maybe in time he will share these things. Maybe not. Even so the dance continues. And as we move forward together, God is transforming us all, perfecting us in love, as John Wesley might have put it. It is a Holy Mystery of the most profoundly sacred proportions. God is making us one, making us whole: one with Christ, one with each other, one in ministry to all the world.

---

*Take our bread, we ask you;*
*take our hearts, we love you,*
*Take our lives, O Father,*
*we are yours, we are yours.*
*Yours as we stand at the table you set;*
*yours as we eat the bread our hearts can't forget.*
*We are the sign of your life with us yet,*
*we are yours, we are yours.*

—Joe Wise, "Take Our Bread"

# "Clergy Health" Is More Than Metrics

*On the verge of fourscore Wesley wrote: "I entered into my eightieth year, but, blessed be God, my time is not labor and sorrow. I find no more pain nor bodily infirmities than at five-and-twenty. This I still impute (1) to the power of God, fitting me for what he calls me to; (2) to my still traveling four or five thousand miles a year; (3) to my sleeping, night or day, whenever I want it; (4) to my rising at a set hour; and (5) to my constant preaching, particularly in the morning." To these he added, "Lastly, evenness of temper. I feel and grieve, but, by the grace of God, I fret at nothing. But still, 'the help that is done upon earth he doeth it himself.' And this he doeth in answer to many prayers."*

—A Methodist Preacher, *John Wesley the Methodist: A Plain Account of His Life and Work*

In the last few years, our denomination has begun to be concerned about the health of its clergy. At the urging of our insurance companies, abysmal indicators of low levels of self-care are being pulled into the spotlight—obesity, high blood pressure, heart disease, and so forth. Not a pretty picture. A number of conferences and pastors have initiated weight-loss contests. Workshops are held on diet and exercise. Blood pressure screenings start with the pastor.

It's all to the good. It's not easy to retain healthful practices when temptation abounds. Especially at the holidays, our dear parishioners express their love in chocolate and sugar concoctions of all sorts. Week in and week out, our erratic schedules lend themselves to fast food and meals on the go. Family dinners around the table become a rare luxury. The stress of the pastoral burden we carry seems to be assuaged by snacking and imbibing. We can feel exhausted, depleted, and literally weighed down. The waistband expands. The pounds accumulate. I joke that there are ten pounds that love me so much that whenever I succeed in shedding them, they simply lurk around, waiting for an opportunity to jump back on.

Our insurance company decided to support the new healthy living campaign by offering us all free pedometers. These little devices are to be strapped onto one's shoe and programmed to count one's steps daily. Awards and prizes are given for the achievement of various step levels. Some colleagues have thrived and love the challenge. A certain competition grew up around the comparison of daily totals. Mine quickly went into a drawer.

My best days begin with a morning walk—thirty minutes, five days a week, my doctor advises. That's a minimum, of course, but it's a goal I can most always achieve. My short-lived pedometer experience revealed to me what I love and cherish about my walks. It's not about the steps. It's about the air, the light, the birds. My walks are a time to look and actually see the glories of God's creation and to be put in my place—both a little lower than the angels and no more significant than my neighbor out walking his dog. It's simultaneously awe-inspiring and totally humbling. My walks are my time to get things off my chest and give them to God. They are time to notice what old energy-sapping tapes the voice in my head has set on endless replay. Enough already. Be silent, you negative, pointless repetitions.

My walks are my time to let new ideas bubble up. I also find that when my mind is free, God often sends people into my awareness. Sometimes that means a pastoral check-in is called for. Sometimes it means that I offer them up to God in prayer for whatever they may be needing that day.

To all who have benefitted from the discipline of the step-counters: more power to you. Walk on! To those like myself who recoil from such contraptions: walk on! The real lesson is in the healthful attributes, the attentiveness, the honoring of the wholeness of body/mind/spirit, however you get there. It's more than metrics. The deeper lessons here are about learning how to love ourselves in healthy ways, how to give of ourselves in ways that are life-affirming rather than self-destructive, how to receive God's gift of life.

Christ came that we might have life and have it abundantly. That means a lot of things. But to be sure, it starts in each of us, and extends to all of God's children in every place. Walk on. Go deep. Reach out. Pray unceasingly.

*Walk with me, and I will walk with you*
*and build the land*
*that God has planned*
*where love shines through.*
*And when you share your faith with me and work*
*for life made new,*
*the witness of your faithfulness*
*calls me to walk with you.*

—John S. Rice, "Walk with Me"

# Friends and Colleagues

*I'm a friend to everyone who honors you*
*and to all who keep your precepts.*

—Psalm 119:63 (CEB)

A priest, a rabbi, and three pastors go into a bar. Truth be told, it's a deli. And it's no joke. Once a month, every month, for years now. We eat and laugh and share things about the work of ministry that need little explanation. We know this crazy vocation from the inside out and the outside in.

You never know in advance where the conversation will go. We don't assign topics or plan an agenda. We simply show up and someone starts talking. We cover theology, personal stuff, scripture, liturgy, administrative challenges, money, sports, Androids versus iPhones, and the weirdest, latest experience of doing God's work in the world.

We're careful to keep confidences and not share names, except in the form of resources and favorite authors. As a result, we can talk through things we could never share with a parishioner and sometimes not even with a spouse. In the best sense of the words, we are professionals and we are friends. We're clear on our boundaries even as we know our deep need for collegiality and companionship around the most challenging things we encounter.

There's an ongoing debate among clergy about whether or not one can have friends in the congregation. I know colleagues who do it well and others who do it badly. Those who do it well move with ease and genuineness between the different roles. They are so authentically who they are, integrated in their faith and practice, that they can both play golf and preside at the funeral service. Those who do it badly run roughshod over emotional boundaries and create a kind of codependency that makes therapists weep.

No matter how friendly or close clergy and parishioners become, there is a role differentiation that persists. There is always another level of relationship. Yes, Jesus gathered his friends around the table that last night. He called them "friends" and he taught them about friendship. But he was always more than one of the guys. To mark this distinction is not to diminish friendship but to honor it while honoring the unique relationship that pastor-parishioner entails as well.

It's hard to pull off congregational friendships without giving the impression of favoritism. While we naturally hit it off more easily with some than others, we are everyone's pastor. The perception that so-and-so has a close relationship with us can be very painful to the person who longs for God's love as embodied in us yet feels cast to some outer circle of intimacy. I suppose I'm old school on this. My view is that in the same way God loves each and every one of us equally, we pastors must strive to convey that same regard to all within our care. Everyone is special and beloved.

However, as a result, we can spend a lifetime being friendly with the countless people with whom we spend our days and nights while still experiencing a deep loneliness. This is a cost of the set-apartness of ordination. After moving to a new community, a colleague once confessed, "I am rich in relationships, but I am without friends."

That's why my little trusted group is so precious to me and so essential to my mental and spiritual health. These are not folks who look to me for anything except for me to be me. There are no transactional aspects to our relationship, except when it's my turn to pick up the breakfast tab. They would not put up for a moment with any whiff of ego or puffery. It's not so much that they keep me honest as that I would never think of being anything but honest in their company. Honest as in totally authentic.

Of course, I have other friends, too. Clergywomen who have shared the long journey of being among the first. Lifelong friends who knew me before ordination. Colleagues from around the church with whom I have worked in a great variety of settings. Leaders and community members closer to home.

There is a dailiness to friendship that is akin to regular exercise and brushing our teeth. It needs that same investment of time and self on our part. One of the worst mistakes we can make in ministry is to be too busy for it. Or to imagine that we can subsist, let alone thrive, without its steadying infusion of regard, love, esteem, perspective, acceptance, and plain-old silliness.

---

*If you want to walk fast, go alone.*
*If you want to go far, walk together with others.*

—African proverb

# The Blessing of
# Peaceful Sleep

---

*Do all the good you can. By all the means you can. In all the ways you can. In
all the places you can. At all the times you can. To all the people you can. As
long as ever you can.*

—Attributed to John Wesley

---

**M**ost pastors experience the curse of knowing we've never done
enough. We Methodists are both blessed and burdened by the
example of our founder, John Wesley. Apparently he was tireless
and driven by the Spirit. For fifty years he traveled forty-five hundred miles
a year and preached an average of twice a day. By the time of his death at the
age of eighty-seven, he had covered more than a quarter of a million miles,
mostly on horseback. He had preached tens of thousands of sermons. These
are the sorts of statistics that still today delight church bureaucrats and pep-
per the pages of countless year-end reports.

The doing, the striving, the relentless sense of more to be done, more
people to be reached, more of God's work to accomplish, permeate his writing. Never mind that his interpersonal relationships, especially with women,
suffered terribly. I think Wesley would have liked to have a Tikker watch.
Created by a young Swedish inventor, the Tikker uses an algorithm like the
one used by insurance companies to determine a person's life expectancy
based on age, country, smoking habits, and gender. Then it counts down,
clicking away the seconds toward one's predicted time of death. Some see
it as morbid. But its creator calls it "The Happiness Watch," intended to
remind the wearer to cherish each remaining moment. Wesley might well
have been driven by his Tikker to do more and more and more as the minutes, hours, and days of his earthly life sped by.

Admittedly, the work of ministry is never done. Daily to-do lists duly
completed can never encompass the ever-present awareness of pastoral calls

that would/should/could have also been done. The additional time that would have made that sermon even more effective. The too frequent experiences of showing up without being fully present, distracted by more and other and nagging responsibilities.

Early in my ministry, I was mentored by a beloved older pastor. He was a gifted preacher and an early advocate for civil rights, risking pulpit and reputation to stand for what was right long before it was popular. He was also funny, gentle, and self-effacing. He was a loving father and a trusted friend. To me, he seemed perfect, just the kind of pastor I longed to become.

Around the time of his retirement, we had a long conversation about his years of ministry. He confessed something I would not have guessed— that he never felt satisfied that he had done enough. In all his years of ministry, he said, he'd never found a way to let it go, to stop and let what he had done be enough. He battled it every night, the knowledge that he could have done more. He had never come to peace with that awareness.

The balance between complacency and acceptance is a tricky one. Having a job where, for large chunks of time each day or week, no one really knows what we're doing, brings with it the temptation to do less than our best. The relentless pressure to achieve impossible benchmarks of numerical success can foster resignation rather than zeal. The lure of a junk-food fix of relentless frenetic activity and busy-ness is ever present. The prodding of one's own self-critical awareness can wear like a hair shirt but also serve as a prod to deeper faithfulness.

Where is peace to be found? Perhaps, circling back around to Wesley, we hear it in his dying words: "The best of all is, God is with us!" The God who is endlessly creating and the God who rests. The God who looks on creation and calls it good. The God who comes not to condemn, but to bring life. The God of whom the psalmist sang: "At day's end I'm ready for sound sleep, / For you, GOD, have put my life back together" (Ps 4:8 *THE MESSAGE*).

Besides, it turns out that Methodist historians now claim that Wesley never said that "Do all the good you can" mantra. Give it a rest.

---

*God, who made the earth and heaven,*
*Darkness and light:*
*You the day for work have given,*

# Carrying the Anxious Weight of the Institutional Church

One of the joys of being a district superintendent was visiting each of my pastors at their church in their office. I wanted to meet them, to know a bit about them and their family, and to see them in their place of ministry. What I soon noticed was that nearly every one of them had on their bookshelf the how-to books of the then current ministry gurus. On the one hand, this could be applauded as an indication of a continuing desire to learn and grow in the practice of ministry. But on the other hand, what I quickly came to sense as well was the panic behind each purchase.

Facing decline in numbers, in dollars, in public prestige and impact, our denominational bodies flail about constantly for anything that will address or fix the problem. New models, new schemes, new techniques. These are pounced upon sequentially by our leaders for implementation on down the production line to us, the line workers whose job it is to produce better numbers or else. What I saw in these how-to books were our own worried questions: Will this work for me? Will I get the promised positive results? Will I be able to turn this place around and reclaim the bustling energy of its heyday?

The actual work of ministry is most often remarkably unremarkable. It involves a daily, weekly discipline of accompanying people through this life. Ministry, to be truly effective, must get up close and personal with all kinds of people through all kinds of life circumstances. No expert is needed to identify these (not listed in any particular order): birth, school, employment, marriage, children, divorce, loneliness, illness, celebration, retirement, loss, faith, doubt, death, sorrow, joy. It's our form of "chop wood, carry water." The daily work we do with our people is the work of ministry. Tuesdays look much like Fridays. And every day, there is wood to be chopped and water to be carried.

The Zen Buddhist might point out, gently, that this is precisely the point. This dailiness is precisely where enlightenment is found, if we're paying attention. Maybe it's part of what Jesus meant when he said "the kingdom of heaven has come near" (Matt 4:17).

Jesus invites us into his ministry of teaching, healing, and preaching good news to people longing for his saving, grace-filled power. That's it. This is the work that transforms lives and transforms the world one hour, one person, one day, one place at a time. I celebrate those moments when an extra-special spark ignites and thousands flock to a particular faith community for a time. But this is the mystery of the work of the Holy Spirit, who gives the gifts and produces the fruits. It is not ours to claim or to achieve. And it need not become an indictment of all who strive to be steadily faithful, usually in much less glamorous ways.

The challenge is to hold onto that place of vocational assurance in our own hearts and self-perception. Are we being faithful in what we have been called to do? The writings of Saint Thérèse of Lisieux point the way. In her "Little Way," she paints a portrait of the spiritual life as not to do extraordinary things, but to do ordinary things extraordinarily well and all for love. "Love is my vocation," she wrote.

Is it possible to simply unstrap that backpack of institutional anxiety that is weighing us down and place it by the side of the road? God will know just what to do with it. It will free us to chop wood and carry water, the quotidian work of ministry, finding there our daily bread, gift of God, in the faces, the hearts, the lives, the souls of those we serve.

---

*Are you tired? Worn out? Burned out on religion? Come to me. Get away with me and you'll recover your life. I'll show you how to take a real rest. Walk with me and work with me—watch how I do it. Learn the unforced rhythms of grace. I won't lay anything heavy or ill-fitting on you. Keep company with me and you'll learn to live freely and lightly.*

—Matthew 11:28-30 (*THE MESSAGE*)

# Sabbath Time

*I leave aside my shoes, my ambitions:*
*undo my watch, my timetable;*
*take off my glasses, my views;*
*unclip my pen, my work;*
*put down my keys, my security;*
*to be alone with you,*
*the only true God.*

—Graham Kings, "The Prayer Stool"

**M**ost of us, too many of us, live at such an incredibly fast pace. We caffeinate regularly. We still can't keep up. All our labor-saving devices and crackerjack techno-gadgets have accelerated the heartbeat of our lives. Everything is compressed into IMs, sound bites, action clips, all designed to squeeze more and more into each ever-smaller bit of time. Instead of saving time, we end up feeling as if life moves too fast. Everything is outpacing us, constantly accelerating, and we are always behind.

We pastors are in it up to our necks with our parishioners. What happens to the time we thought we were saving? There's never enough time in the day, no matter how ramped up we are. Not enough days in the week. Not enough weeks in the month. Not enough months in the year. Not enough years to enjoy our kids, to fish all the greatest trout streams, to see all the places we want to see, to read all the books, to try all the recipes, to get to all those things on our "bucket list," the things to be sure to do before kicking the bucket.

Jesus gives clues. In this, too, his Way proves to be a healthy and salvific Way for us. To be sure, he seems to be pretty good at multitasking. He was, after all, a young adult in the heyday of his ministry years. Like all youth and young adults, he could do a lot of things at once. He could recruit and teach and heal and preach and travel and take in what was going on around him and see through tricky attempts to catch him off guard pretty much simultaneously.

Sometimes he actually sat down and gathered everyone around him and taught in something of a classroom style. But usually Jesus was teaching on the go, in the midst of whatever the day had brought, to whoever would listen, for whoever had an ache in their heart or a question in their soul. Jesus had a way of focusing in, of paying attention. His intuition was always ratcheted up to "high" and in the midst of lots going on around him, he could key in to the needful thing. In this, he could teach his disciples, too: "Pay attention to what you hear." Pay attention. Pay attention. And the truth of God's love and power and beauty and faithfulness will ever so slowly but surely be revealed to you.

One time he talked to them about the mustard seed, the smallest of seeds, that grows into the greatest of all shrubs, and that's just what the kingdom of God is like. Really? Not a majestic tree. Not a magnificent flower. No. A bush. A shrub. True, Jesus calls it the greatest of all shrubs, but still it's only a shrub. And yet, he says, that is what the kingdom of God is like. The greatest of all shrubs, with large branches, so that the birds of the air can nest in its shade.

The branches of the kingdom of God provide that same safe space for us all, a place to nest and find new life. "Pay attention," Jesus says to us. Slow down. Take a deep breath. Focus on one thing at a time. Otherwise you might race right past that very ordinary old bush and not notice the rest and new life available for you in the quiet beauty of its shade.

Jesus invites us into this Way of being in the world in order that we might refocus, reconsider our priorities and our use of time, reflect on all that is or should be most important in our lives, hear more clearly God's will and deepest desires for us, and perceive God's dreams for this world. Our own hubris and drivenness get in the way. We imagine ourselves to be indispensable. We sense that if we stop running, it might all come crashing down around us. We fear that what we would see, the results of all our efforts, would not measure up or be found worthy.

We need to intentionally stop, regularly. To create Sabbath times, in our week, our month, our year. To take time for continuing our learning and going deep in prayer. Time to simply be, to pay attention, and to know.

Jesus offers peace. Rest in the shade of the bush. Abide in the safety of its branches.

---

*Be still and know that I am God*
*Be still and know that I am*
*Be still and know that*
*Be still and know*
*Be still and*
*Be still*
*Be*

—Mpho Tutu

# Prophet

# Stepping Up

*Now the boy Samuel was ministering to the Lord under Eli. The word of the Lord was rare in those days; visions were not widespread. At that time Eli, whose eyesight had begun to grow dim so that he could not see, was lying down in his room; the lamp of God had not yet gone out, and Samuel was lying down in the temple of the Lord, where the ark of God was. Then the Lord called, "Samuel! Samuel!" and he said, "Here I am!" and ran to Eli, and said, "Here I am, for you called me." But he said, "I did not call; lie down again." So he went and lay down. The Lord called again, "Samuel!" Samuel got up and went to Eli, and said, "Here I am, for you called me." But he said, "I did not call, my son; lie down again." Now Samuel did not yet know the Lord, and the word of the Lord had not yet been revealed to him. The Lord called Samuel again, a third time. And he got up and went to Eli, and said, "Here I am, for you called me." Then Eli perceived that the Lord was calling the boy. Therefore Eli said to Samuel, "Go, lie down; and if he calls you, you shall say, 'Speak, Lord, for your servant is listening.'" So Samuel went and lay down in his place. Now the Lord came and stood there, calling as before, "Samuel! Samuel!" And Samuel said, "Speak, for your servant is listening."*

—1 Samuel 3:1-10

I came into ordained ministry at a time of tremendous social movements—the peace movement, the civil rights movement, the student movement, the women's movement. I don't regret that for a moment. My involvement in those causes in various ways had taught me the power of organizing as well as the commitment to seek change. I had experienced firsthand the exhilaration of working together to change the world.

The one downside, as I reflect on it now, was perhaps a diminished sense of the power of one, that is, the impact we are each called to make. If one's norms are collaboration, solidarity, and nonhierarchical shared leadership, stepping up as a leader feels egotistical. Not wanting to be seen as what my Aussie friends call "a tall poppy," I held back. I waited. I demurred. All for the right reasons, understandable reasons, but reasons that kept me from claiming the fullness of my power and from stepping into my role as a leader.

These things were hard to unlearn. Stepping out in leadership did not feel comfortable. It did not feel like "me." Yet ministry calls us, even authorizes us, to lead. Moreover, the church and the work of kingdom building itself call forth leaders. We are called to lead in ways that are clear, impactful, and faithful, ways that empower others and invite them into their own sphere of leadership, their own voice as well.

We can see this in the story of God's call of the young boy Samuel. We can see it in the life of Martin Luther King Jr., whose example and teachings we do well to revisit at least annually on the federal holiday commemorating his birthday. When we think of King as a great orator, as a movement leader, as a Nobel Prize recipient, we may forget that he was a reluctant leader. When asked by others to lead the Montgomery boycott in 1958, he was only twenty-six years old. He had just been married for two years. It was dangerous. He was a brand-new pastor. Most significantly, perhaps, he doubted his own speaking skills, his ability to inspire a crowd, his ability to lead. He prayed, and then he jumped in.

Nation, world, and church are eternally grateful that he did. We've come such a long way now. And while enormous challenges and obstacles still lie ahead, who could measure where we would be today if Martin Luther King Jr. had not claimed the power of one, and then added his gifts to those of others to draw forth a more beautiful dream.

We cannot know in advance where and when our leadership will be essential. We cannot know what gifts we will need, nor find any guarantee that we will be up to the task. But we can prepare ourselves by serving anyway, as did the young boy Samuel. We can prepare by surrounding ourselves with wise and experienced mentors like the old Eli. We can prepare by listening in the night for the voice of God, the still quiet voice, most likely, that whispers and nudges and opens our eyes, ears, and hearts to more than we had perceived.

---

*GOD promises to love me all day,*
*sing songs all through the night!*
*My life is God's prayer.*

—Psalm 42:8b (*THE MESSAGE*)

# The Newspaper
# and the Bible

---

*We have the world to live in on the condition that we will take good care of it. And to take good care of it, we have to know it. And to know it and to be willing to take care of it, we have to love it.*

—Wendell Berry

---

The great German theologian Karl Barth insisted that the church approach faith and theology with the Bible in one hand and the newspaper in the other. I was blessed to grow up in a congregation that took this to heart. As youth, we were plunged into the hot issues of our day—racism and poverty in America. I still marvel at the preparation that was required of us prior to our participation in a summer "mission of the church" tour. We read *The Autobiography of Malcolm X* and *The Other America*, and then went off to visit and reflect theologically on the tutoring programs of the Black Panthers in Los Angeles, the struggles of the farmworkers San Francisco. For a kid from Arizona, this was wild and crazy stuff. The fact that my eyes were being opened through the lens of faith and church made all the difference in the world.

John Wesley got it. The spiritual practices adopted by his college group at Oxford, those first strange "Methodists" who insisted on a very disciplined life of prayer, sacrament, and study, included regular visits to the neighboring prison as well. As the movement grew, Wesley wisely insisted that his Methodists engage in consistent weekly work directly with the poor, both for the sake of the poor and for the sake of the spiritual health of the Methodist people. He knew that in order for the poor not to be stereotyped, romanticized, marginalized, or demonized, direct personal relationships were required. As he observed:

> One reason why the rich in general have so little sympathy for the
> poor is because they so seldom visit them. Hence it is that, according

to the common observation, one part of the world does not know what the other suffers. Many of them do not know, because they do not care to know: they keep out of the way of knowing it—and then plead their voluntary ignorance as an excuse for their hardness of heart. ("On Visiting the Sick")

It's a challenge to avoid the "voluntary ignorance" pull in ministry. Understandably, people come to church to step out of the madness and pain of the world to find some moments of peace and renewal. Most of us don't choose to be made to feel uncomfortable or guilty. Still, as the saying goes, it's our job to comfort the afflicted and afflict the comfortable, in the manner of Jesus. Wrestling with the assigned lectionary texts helps, as the scriptures themselves have a way of pointing us to the needs of the world. Take, for example, Jesus's words to the rich young ruler seeking to inherit eternal life: "Sell what you own, and give the money to the poor. . . . And come follow me" (Matt 19:21–22 CEB). Those words alone should set us back an hour or two on a Sunday afternoon.

Still and all, nothing does it like hands-on mission. It takes us to the heart of the incarnation and reveals where God is made flesh and in whom. Actual human relationships, heart-to-heart, help keep us from getting so caught up in our own stuff that we fail to see everyone not as an object of our mission outreach, but as a child of God.

I still thank in my prayers the youth minister who was brave and bold enough to make our mission tour happen, and the senior minister who backed him up when some of the church elders found it all to be more than a bit too much. Long before I could recognize God calling me into ordained ministry, I learned just how exciting and demanding it is to engage the world in all its brokenness and messiness for the love of God.

Generations of youth continue to be transformed through participation in the Appalachia Service Project and its sobering immersion into poverty, not so different from that described in *The Other America* fifty years ago. They come back with a million questions, eyes wide open, hearts broken in the sacrament of self-giving love, voluntary ignorance no longer an option. "I had no idea," one said as she reported back to the congregation, thanking them for their love and support. "It's so wrong. I don't know yet what all this means for my life, but I will never forget what I saw and the people we met. We saw God there."

*A pilgrim on a pilgrimage*
*Walked across the Brooklyn Bridge*
*His sneakers torn*
*In the hour when the homeless move their cardboard blankets*
*And the new day is born*
*Folded in his backpack pocket*
*The questions that he copied from his heart*
*Who am I in this lonely world?*
*And where will I make my bed tonight?*
*When twilight turns to dark*

*. . . . . . . . . . . .*

*Questions for the angels*
*Who believes in angels?*
*I do*
*Fools and pilgrims all over the world*

—Paul Simon, "Questions for the Angels"

# Learning to Disagree (Deeply)

---

*Christians ought to be able to disagree well together.*

—Justin Welby, Archbishop of Canterbury

---

A parishioner once told me that although she knew she and I were most likely poles apart politically, she trusted me as her pastor. For her, that was unwavering. To my ears, this is in the "ultimate compliment" category. I understand church to be a place where we learn how to bring the depths of our convictions to the table, to agree sometimes and at other times learn how to disagree well together. Church is not about groupthink on matters temporal and political.

I come to this from a deeply theological understanding. God gave us minds and wants us to use our minds. Moreover, we are commanded to love God with all our minds. That means we don't check our minds at the door of the sanctuary. We don't worship together despite our different points of view on a whole manner of things. Rather, we worship together a God who is so much bigger than all our labels and categories and boxes and still manages to make clear that we are loved, each and every one. Created in the image of that God, we are called to strive to the same generosity of spirit.

This is hard work and part of the job description of a disciple. There is no indication in scripture that Jesus chose the twelve because they had passed a litmus test on the top ten key issues of the day. In fact, he seems to spend a good deal of time coaching them on how to love each other and serve him in spite of their differences in personality and approach. And he gave his church the way to remember him, to experience him afresh in every moment, in the compelling symbols of one loaf and one cup.

Some of us learn how to do this around the dinner table growing up. Family time is a time when we are encouraged to speak our minds and to listen in love to another's viewpoint. Many of us, however, have grown up in a different model. The family dinner table is a place of silence, lest order be shaken. We learned to keep our own counsel and not rock the boat. I'm no family systems expert, but I have a strong sense that what we learned about these things in our own families is what we bring to our experiences of church. Are we comfortable with frank and open sharing? Can we have it out with one another and still enjoy dessert together? Or do we cringe and shy away, sensing that the peace, once broken, may never be restored?

For those who are uncomfortable with honest expressions of diversity, it's no wonder that church is supposed to be a place where troubling issues are never explored. Peace at all costs comes to resemble the peace of the dead. When such is the norm in a community of faith, it takes time, care, and patience to help people become comfortable engaging one another openly and honestly. It's best done in small groups, in study forums, in scripture classes. People need to feel safe and loved unconditionally. This is why I hardly ever approach the pulpit as a bully pulpit, except to constantly hammer home the fundamentals of God's love, justice, peace, and care for the least and the lost.

The art of learning how to respect one another across political divides is also a gift of the church to our larger society and political arena. Polarization that stifles compromise most often extracts the highest toll from those least able to afford it. The marginalized, the poor, the disenfranchised only suffer more when pontification replaces reasoned political discourse. Democracy itself suffers and the great American experiment is placed in peril.

To be clear, the community of faith is not to be a community of apathy, indifference, or live-and-let-live. It is to be a vibrant, engaged microcosm of the people of God where, in the Pentecost model, each speaks their own language and all hear and understand. I like to imagine the Holy Spirit standing by, ready to engage, eager to open our hearts and minds and correct us when we are tempted to bear false witness against one another in pursuit of our own shortsighted aims. The rainbow arc of God's everlasting covenant fills the sky of the whole creation and encompasses all within its span.

---

*Your love, O God, is broad like beach and meadow,*
*wide as the wind, and our eternal home.*

—Anders Frostenson, "Your Love, O God"

# Seeing the Truth in One's Opponent

*What troubles have we seen,*
*what mighty conflicts past,*
*fightings without, and fears within,*
*since we assembled last!*

—Charles Wesley, "And Are We Yet Alive"

'm not a John Wesley scholar. With my not coming from a long line of Methodists and not attending a United Methodist seminary, it's actually rather funny that I taught United Methodist history at one of our seminaries for a couple years. I loved the students. And almost as much, I loved the things I learned about Wesley that occasionally knocked my socks off.

For example, Wesley liked to define *pride* in terms of not seeing that your opponent, or someone you seriously disagree with, as having something to teach you. In fact, he thought it vitally important to listen to that very person in order to learn what you didn't know that you didn't know. Otherwise, you were guilty of pride.

Beyond mere humility, important in and of itself, Wesley pushed his Methodists toward a deep level of listening and respect precisely with those whose views we find to be most obnoxious or disreputable. What a refreshing change this would bring to the kind of shouting that parades itself these days as political discourse. But his approach was no less remarkable in his own time, when debates over points of theology filled newspapers and more often than not resulted in the presence of menacing mobs at public sermons. Wesley went at it with the best of them, which makes it all the more fascinating to learn that rather than vilifying his opponents, he recognized a certain common humanity, and he honestly owned up to the tendency within himself to dismiss out of hand the very views that would shed light on the gaping holes in our own logic and the error of our ways.

Granted, Wesley proved to be more adept at applying this insight on the theological level than on the very practical level of life in Christian community. In fact, his approach to ministry itself could be described as much more authoritarian than collaborative, to be sure. That's OK. The wisdom is ours to embrace and apply.

A number of years ago, I became embroiled in congregational conflict that nearly did me in. It was mean and hurtful. It was confounding and irrational. And at first I succumbed to all the available temptations to hunker down, assume the role of victim, and dismiss those who disagreed with me. Right/wrong. Win/lose. These were the frameworks I fell into thoughtlessly.

As Wesley clearly knew, an exaggerated sense of one's own worth is a terrible and dangerous thing, for it's built on the premise of one's superiority over another. Individuals do it. Nations do it. In fact, we are so prone to thinking better of ourselves than we ought that we don't even realize that we're doing it until we feel so entitled to harbor these inflated notions about ourselves that our arrogance and pride is hidden from us and seems quite natural. Eventually the need that we have to find fault with another, to point out another's brokenness and sin, overshadows our need to confess our own.

And so, needless to say perhaps, our congregation quickly got nowhere, except worse. Fortunately, with the advice of counseling and coaching, and a good deal of self-reflection, the truth of Wesley's caution hit home. I took more than a few deep breaths and sat down to make lists. I first listed their concerns as straightforwardly as I could. I could then reflect on where I thought they were right on. I could see where their concerns contradicted themselves, revealing a range of opinions rather than a coordinated attack. And I began to see the areas in which there was simply general misunderstanding of initiatives that had been taken.

This process opened me up to be able see what I needed to learn from all that "they" were saying. As a result, I learned a lot about myself. What wasn't working. What wasn't communicating. Where I needed to step up and where I needed to back off. What people just plain didn't understand about what I was trying to do and why. What was "them" and what was "me." What might have been expected at this point in our relationship and how to create a new path into the future. Perhaps the most wondrous thing about it all was that many of those relationships healed in time and are even much stronger today. We all learned how to give, how to take, how to offer, how to receive, how to share our fears, how to name our hope.

At some point along the way, I remembered some training in nonviolent action that I'd experienced years ago. It was predicated, of course, on nonviolence of word and nonviolence of deed and added nonviolence of thought and nonviolence of heart. Maybe this was the most important lesson of all—to disarm the heart in order to make space for new truth and new life.

---

*And are we yet alive,*
*and see each other's face?*
*Glory and thanks to Jesus give*
*for his almighty grace!*

—Charles Wesley, "And Are We Yet Alive"

# Pointing to Hope

*What on earth is going on in my heart*
*Has it turned as cold as stone*
*Seems these days I don't feel anything*
*Less it cuts me right down to the bone*
*What on earth is going on in my heart*

—David Gray, "My Oh My"

Columbine, Tucson, Newtown. These place names, the photos of the dead, the anguish of those left behind, the solemn memorials as well as the spontaneous crowd-sourced shrines, these are the place markers of the last several years in the life of our nation. Can our broken hearts still weep? How can we focus our rage? What pulls us back to pain when we'd prefer numbness and escape?

When a lone gunman entered the Sandy Hook Elementary School in Newtown, Connecticut, and shot twenty-seven children and teachers at point-blank range, it seemed as though we might have reached some tipping point. Surely this horrific violence would shake us back alive to the possibilities of gun safety legislation, stricter background checks, prohibitions on (multishot) weapons. Speeches were made. Promises, too. Vows of "never again."

In worship, we prayed. We sang. We shook our heads and hugged. We held on to the children and cherished their laughter all the more deeply. In our preschool, we reviewed safety measures. Wrote new protocols for horrors we desperately hoped to never need. We risked reaching across our own political divides to talk openly with one another, to begin to fashion, however haltingly, a new safety net of restraint and compassion. Surely something new was possible.

And then a staff member texted me on June 7, 2013. Shootings in Santa Monica. I was out of town and immediately turned around to head home. At first, there was so much we did not know and no one could say. How many? Who? In those early hours of sound bites, speculation, bits and pieces of news, we held our breath. We wept. Did we know them? Were they one of ours? Was it over?

As the details emerged, so much was nauseatingly familiar. Gunman in his twenties. Mental issues. Semiautomatic weapon. High-capacity magazine. Innocent bystanders in the line of fire. The stories. The faces. The tears. Again.

I was not prepared for the e-mails and comments that began to come. The very people who a few short months prior had felt the hope of change had been beaten down. If nothing was changed by Newtown, they asked, why should we think anything will change this time? We will bury our dead and hunker down. And we will stop believing that tomorrow's tomorrow would ever be a better day.

My vocation was never clearer. After all, our congregation, after Hurricane Katrina, had adopted the theme "Be the Hope." It had happened gradually. Early on it was a way to galvanize our fund-raising and missional outreach to the people of New Orleans. But gradually, we saw that it spoke truth in more and more situations. Those three words, "Be the Hope," began to define us and how we thought of God and how we saw ourselves as God's faithful ones.

The June shootings in our town did not just break our hearts but tested our faith. To the core. We had to dig deep into the words of the psalmists and the prophets and the evangelists. We had to push ourselves to grow up into an even more mature conviction. We had to call each other back from the brink of cynicism, a snare of the tempter if there ever was one, to the crazy, superrational, unfettered hope that is the good news at the heart of the good news. Otherwise, none of it makes any sense.

Centuries ago, our ancestors in faith, Shadrach, Meshach, and Abednego, said it in the book of Daniel. Threatened with the fiery furnace, they defiantly testified to King Nebuchadnezzar, "If we are thrown into the blazing furnace, the God we serve is able to deliver us from it, and he will deliver us from Your Majesty's hand. But *even if he does not*, we want you to know, Your Majesty, that we will not serve your gods or worship the image of gold you have set up" (Dan 3:17-18 NIV, emphasis added).

It's that "even if not" phrase that sets our resolve. This is how we resist the snares of resignation and despair. And in God and in one another we will find the love to keep us pushing on. Anyway.

*What on earth is going on in my head*
*You know I used to be so sure*
*You know I used to be so definite*
*Thought I knew what love was for*
*I look around these days and I'm not so sure*

. . . . . . . . . . . . . . . . .

*It takes a lotta love*
*It takes a lotta love my friend*
*To keep your heart from freezing*
*To push on till the end*

—David Gray, "My Oh My"

# Make Way for the Image of the Holy One

Our interfaith journey began in earnest shortly after the attacks on the World Trade Center towers in New York City in September of 2001. Well, that's not entirely true. Our congregation had hosted a neighbor synagogue needing expanded space for its High Holy Day services for many years. We delighted in their presence, especially relishing astonished calls from members and neighbors reporting large numbers of men wearing yarmulkes going in and out of the sanctuary. "Oh, those guys . . . yes . . . they are here to pray."

In the aftermath of 9/11, it became abundantly clear that the polite, formal interfaith relationships which existed in the community, primarily limited to the clergy, needed to grow broad and deep. We had a lot to learn about each other. More importantly, we needed to build trust and a new foundation from which to stand together in the face of reactive prejudice and fear.

We started with conversations, expressions of concern and caring, and moved to panel discussions and presentations. We visited each other's places of worship. We shared meals. All the while the right-wing media was fomenting hatred and fear. That poisonous message was heard by many, including some within the congregation, who saw our efforts as naïve or misguided. We carried on, studying, meeting, talking.

After a time, all that seemed to subside somewhat. The intensity dissipated and interest waned as we, nation and congregation, settled back into "the new normal." But in 2011 the tenth anniversary of the attacks became an occasion to crank up the media assault, to open the old wounds. We saw that we had not moved very far down the path of true understanding, respect, and solidarity.

The conversations resumed in earnest. To mark the anniversary, we created a service called "Interfaith Prayers for Peace," which we held in our sanctuary, led by Christian, Jewish, and Muslim clergy colleagues. More of our members came than I would ever have imagined. For that hour, our hearts and souls were united in prayer, our earnest intentions for peace and respect given voice and visibility. And again we shared food.

A hunger for more followed in the wake of that prayer service. Working with my colleague from the Islamic Center of Southern California, we gathered together a group, ten from his congregation, ten from ours, to meet over seven months. The Muslim participants were all folks who live and work right in our community, though we had not known one another prior. For seven months we studied each other's holy texts and traditions. We became friends and eagerly shared family photos. Our kids became friends in child care. We stood by one another during illnesses and births. No question was out of bounds. We learned to trust and to love. One Muslim participant said she felt it a blessing and an experience that would change her life. A Christian member called it a privilege and an honor. It was holy time and sacred space.

That group experience concluded with prayers and a wonderful feast at the Islamic Center. But new seeds had been planted. Our Muslim neighbors and new-found friends had shared that there was no location in the vicinity to gather for Friday prayers. Lunchtime work schedules rarely permitted them to make the round-trip to the Islamic Center downtown. How about our space, we asked ourselves? Do you think we could make it work?

It did not take long to negotiate the particulars of moving chairs and of facilities for washing before prayer. All that remained was discussion in the church council, chaired by a young father who had been part of the seven-month experience. The discussion was lively and loving. Would they need this or that? How could we make them feel truly welcome? When the vote was called, it was unanimous. "Shouldn't everyone have a place to pray?" a member observed.

Now each Friday, some twenty-five neighbors come for prayer. Anyone is invited. The prayers are in Arabic, the sermon in English. The message often sounds much like what one might hear on Sunday morning in the sanctuary. As we study and pray together, we continue to learn how we are alike and where we are different and how those differences enrich the tapestry of life.

After the first year together, the Friday coordinator wrote: "As always, I pray that God rewards you and your family abundantly for your work and good deeds . . . I pray everyone in your church is blessed with the love and guidance of God and I continue to feel so blessed for the opportunity to share my prayers in the church on Fridays."

There are many ways to witness to the love of God, and the world is hungry for our witness. We need but open the door and take the first step. There are new friends to be found and the ever-beckoning wideness of God's love to explore. And there is prayer to be prayed together, in many ways, in multiple languages, heart to heart, child of God with child of God.

---

*Rabbi Joshua ben Levi said: "A procession of angels pass before each person, and the heralds go before them, saying, 'Make way for the image of God!'"*

—Deut. Rabbah, 4:4

# Pilgrim

# Where the Ministry
# Is Leading Us

*There are two things to do about the Gospel—believe it and behave it.*

—Susannah Wesley

I am a terrible chess player. I'm totally reactive, responding to one move at a time. I can't read my opponent's mind to know what they're going to do, and I can't see ten, twenty, fifty moves ahead to know how the game will come out even as it starts. Sometimes I think this is because I don't think spatially. I can drive somewhere, but if asked for directions, my brain freezes. I can't see the map in my mind's eye, let alone describe to someone how to navigate it.

This is a problem for someone in ministry in these times, not because we're supposed to be playing chess on a regular basis, but because we're supposed to have a strategic plan for everything. We're supposed to have a vision statement, a mission statement, and a one-, five-, or ten-year plan with deliverables and measurable goals. As I look back over my years in ministry, I have quite a few of these filed away—plans for the local church, plans for the larger church, plans for a year of my own ministry.

I know enough to know not to pooh-pooh this all together. It works for some. Maybe it works for many or for most. I myself am even good with short-term plans. People tease me about the plans and lists I create to make it through each day. They rarely play out the way I'd envisioned, but I'm comforted by having a plan. But the fact that so very often my days do not actually go according to plan is perhaps why I'm skeptical of putting a lot of time and energy into the big institutional ones. Ministry happens. Life happens. As has been noted, "Life is what happens to you while you're busy making other plans."

Fortunately I have lived and served long enough to be experiencing part of the revitalization of the church through new forms of ministry—missional church, emerging church, and so forth. These models are organic and relational, which is how I do ministry, too. Missional living, a rule of life, spiritual practices—these are the hallmarks and watchwords of the day. Ministry emerges out of where God is leading. Deep discernment is required that involves reading the signs of times, listening to the heartbeat of the people, and quietly waiting for the leading of the Holy Spirit. We're called to prayer rather than to PowerPoint and Sharpies.

Although the various forms of these movements are new, their roots are ancient and constitutive of the People of the Way. While there are those who might argue that Jesus proceeded with a plan, my sense is that he was deeply imbued with the Spirit of the kingdom of God such that ministry trajectories unfolded naturally from his teaching, preaching, and healing. He instructed his followers to do the same. "Follow me," he said. What's important is what happens on the Way.

In reflecting on current ministry initiatives in the life of our congregation, it's hard to imagine how the most vital of them would have been born from planning processes. In contrast, they grew out of the need of the moment and the resources available. Hence, ministries such as the children's after-school theater program, hosting Friday Muslim prayers, or the prayer quilt ministry were not envisioned, strategized, and implemented on a timeline with measurable goals. They grew out of the fertile interaction between the longings of the people and the community and the gifts of leadership offered by clergy and laity alike.

It's not that there's no value in a plan. A sanctuary could not be built without detailed plans. But a church? That's something else all together. A church grows in human lives, through opportunities recognized and dreams dreamed and embraced. Hence, while knowing our need for local, hands-on mission involvement that families could participate in together, we chose to participate in a new walk-a-thon to raise money for homeless families. The fact that it was happening on a Sunday morning first seemed to make it a non-starter. The Spirit helped us see this as an opportunity for witness and for worship—praying with our feet, in the manner of Abraham Joshua Heschel. Our group, sporting our church T-shirts, gathers for Holy Communion and walks together. Teaching, preaching, healing by our lives, with our feet.

The prophet said it—your young will see visions and your old folk will dream dreams when the Holy Spirit is poured out upon them (Joel 2:28). Stay grounded. Pray unceasingly. Be nimble on your feet. And follow the One who is the Way, the Truth, and the Life.

---

*If you love something, it will work.*
*That's the only rule.*

—Bunny Williams, interior designer

# With All Due Haste

*Again I saw that under the sun the race is not to the swift, nor the battle to the strong, nor bread to the wise, nor riches to the intelligent, nor favor to the skillful; but time and chance happen to them all.*

—Ecclesiastes 9:11

Aesop's fable "The Tortoise and Hare" recounts the story of a slow, lumbering tortoise who, having been badgered by a swift-running hare, challenges him to race. The hare speeds ahead. The tortoise moves methodically along. The hare becomes so confident of a win that he stops mid-race for a nap, followed by breakfast and another nap. The tortoise just keeps on moving, slowly but steadily, crossing the finish line in front of the flabbergasted hare. Smiling, the tortoise looks at the hare and comments, "Slowly does it every time."

There are many styles of ministry and many approaches to the life-giving change inherent in every generation of the church's life. I am in awe of colleagues who can sweep into a new situation with a full-blown plan already in mind and move mountains in mere months. I have seen instances when this has worked really well, awakening moribund communities and infusing them with new purpose and mission. I have seen this done badly as well, where the zeal for change at any cost left many old saints sputtering in the dust, feelings hurt, memories bruised, trust broken.

If my fleet-minded colleagues are ministry hares, I am of the tortoise family. I move slowly into new communities, listening, observing, taking the pulse. I immerse myself in stories, history, context. I look for openings. I paint dreams. I point to roadblocks and to open doors.

There's nothing inherently good or bad in fast or slow. Clearly, the devil is in the details, an expression derived from the original "God is in the details." Careful discernment is necessary for the faithful practice of ministry, neither too fast nor too slow. Not one for strategic plans and measurable goals, I can miss the moment. I can be excessively cautious. I can overthink a situation. I, too, can be lulled into napping when I ought to be pressing on. But still, I go for slow, for deep roots and open hearts. Growth happens, with all due haste, and God willing, it is deep and long-lived. Respectful, showing honor and care, animated by an underlying pulse of holy urgency.

My all-time favorite example of the fruits-of-the-tortoise approach came with a bittersweet flavor to it. I had at last taken a three-month renewal leave. While our polity provides for this, I had not taken advantage of this gift until almost three decades of full-time ministry had passed. It was lovely and rich, and I was sure that the congregation had missed me very much. When we gathered as a church council after I'd returned to reflect and debrief, no one had much to say. They were glad to see me, but clearly the ministry had thrived. Truth be told, I was a little hurt. Until another leader observed astutely, "Isn't this what you've been working toward all these years? A church where the ministry belongs to the congregation, is led by the congregation?" Honestly, in that moment, I didn't know whether to laugh or cry. Now I laugh, like Sarah laughed. Who could be more tortoise-like than Sarah, and a God who abides patiently, yet insistently, and awaits the moment? And when the moment comes, it comes with a holy laugh.

A similar tale could be told of our long journey toward full inclusion of our gay and lesbian brothers and sisters. Our congregation has made the journey slowly, which has caused pain to those eager for change and some measure of assurance to those who feared or opposed it. We are indebted to those who pushed harder, who spoke to the truth of their own lives and families, impatient to see justice where justice has long been denied. We have moved at a measured pace in the hope of bringing more people along, giving the heart its own time to soften and giving time for the brain to catch up with the heart.

We moved with all due haste, with diligence and single-mindedness, prodded by a nagging sense of urgency and incompleteness. And when the time finally came for official action, we were able to vote unanimously to simply state that all the ministries of the church are open to all God's children. "Isn't this what Jesus would want?" someone asked. And we hugged and cried and then began to laugh together, for it seemed so clear in hindsight that God had been guiding us all along the Way. Looking back, it was impossible to see how in the world it could have taken us so long to catch up. We could but laugh at ourselves and at the amazing tenacity of our

God, who loves us all as we are, never settling for less than what we are yet to become.

"You have all the time you need," our Buddhist brothers and sisters would say.

---

*Guide my feet, while I run this race. For I don't want to run this race in vain.*
*Hold my hand . . . I'm your child . . . Stand by me . . .*
*Search my heart . . . while I run this race,*
*for I don't want to run this race in vain.*

—African-American spiritual

# An Elastic and Inquisitive Mind

---

*Every day I make an effort to go toward what I don't understand.*

—Yo-Yo Ma

---

I t is abundantly clear to me that in so many ways life is passing me by at an increasingly accelerated pace. I have been urged to write a blog, for example. I don't read anyone else's blog so it seems quite presumptuous to think that someone should take the time to read mine. And with over 150+ million blogs already out there in cyberspace, would one more truly contribute anything to the accumulated wisdom of humankind? Or am I missing the point? I don't know.

"Social media catches up with you anyway," a friend of mine told me when I confessed that I have no idea how Pinterest works. "Don't worry," she said. So I try not to worry, but I do wonder. A lot. Mostly I try and maintain a healthy curiosity about this wild and wonderful world that God has created/is creating. Some learnings reassure, like the evidence that dark chocolate is good for you in a variety of ways. Other facts are just plain awe-inspiring, such as knowing that there are many more planets than stars out there in space. Who knew? And what might be happening on any one or two, or one or two hundred of them, at this very moment?

Maintaining an inquisitive mind is key to longevity in ministry, or at least to continuing to truly love the wonders and challenges it presents day in and day out. People are endlessly fascinating and wondrous. Their yearnings, longings and needs, while in some ways universal, are simultaneously exquisitely personal and unique. I love hearing a question I've never heard before, something that catches me up short and causes me to reflect before offering a cookie-cutter response. I frequently discover that new members, particularly young adults, are engaged in work I've never heard of let alone know anything about, like experiential advertising and digital media supervising.

Some years ago, a member of the congregation confessed to me, with no small amount of trepidation in her voice, that she was reading a book by Bishop John Shelby Spong. She was really fascinated by it and drawn in to the new insights and connections he was offering. But, she questioned, "*Should* I be reading this?" as if she had transgressed by reading something controversial and edgy, theologically speaking. "Of course," I said. "Read it and think for yourself."

That one conversation which lasted only a minute or so led me to initiate a monthly book group, which continues. United Methodists are called to the theological work of renewing our theology in every generation. We take seriously the commandment to love God with all our minds, as well as all our souls and strength. I intentionally choose books for us to read that will challenge our established ways of thinking or open up new ways of seeing the world and our place in it.

Having an inquisitive mind keeps the preaching task life-giving as well. I intentionally use sermon preparation as time to read new work on scripture, and more often than not some new insight will appear in a passage I've read a million times. That's why it's scripture, I am constantly reminded. It is God's living word of life and there is no end to its scope and depth or of the ways it speaks to our human condition. My goal is to keep opening God's word in ways that shine new light, carry new hope, prod with new urgency, or sing a new song.

"Be transformed by the renewing of your minds," Paul said (Rom 12:2). Apparently the one-terabyte flash drive can store all the libraries of the world. Makes me wonder how big our minds can grow? How large is the mind of God? How many new things await our contemplation? I'm not so much interested in the answers to those questions as in all the fun and joy there is to be experienced exploring the path.

---

*Do not let my world grow old.*

—Martin Buber

# Stability

---

*And Ruth said, Intreat me not to leave thee, or to return from following after thee: for whither thou goest, I will go; and where thou lodgest, I will lodge: thy people shall be my people, and thy God my God.*

—Ruth 1:16 (KJV)

---

Clergy aren't necessarily known for the Benedictine hallmark of stability, especially United Methodists, itinerant as we are. We descend from John Wesley's line of circuit riders, saddle bags always packed, unencumbered by property or spouse, and most certainly allergic to planting our own flag or name on the church we are appointed to serve. John's own brother, Charles, though, established another model of ministry right from the get-go. Happily married, he settled down.

What does it mean in our time to declare allegiance to the place and people we serve? I'll leave the administrative details of all this to bishops and superintendents. But there's something vital at stake here, something that goes to the heart of incarnation. After all, as John says in his Gospel, "The Word became flesh and blood, / and moved into the neighborhood" (1:14 *THE MESSAGE*). Things are different in other parts of the country, to be sure. But in my neighborhood, people come and go all the time now. Young adults are here for a season until the next job opportunity presents itself. Young families are here until they want a house with a yard that they can afford. The middle class has been squeezed out by exorbitant property values. The seniors are here until they are called home above.

I want to plant my flag here in this community in a way that says that the church is a place you can count on as you come and go. The church is a place that is looking out for the well-being of this place. The church is not going to pack up and leave next week when something brighter beckons. The church is going to honor the people who used to be here and serve the people who are here for a time and make sure things are in place and good for the people yet to come.

I keep a woodblock print of Jonah inside the whale hanging in my office to remind me of these things. Eugene Peterson has written evocatively of Jonah's temptation to want, so very badly, to go to Tarshish rather than to Nineveh. Tarshish was the happening place. It was an exotic, exciting port city, where ships arrived with things like gold and monkeys and ivory and peacocks. I can imagine this Tarshish, having lived for a year in the Mediterranean port city of Marseille. There I saw Greeks and gypsies, Arabs and Africans, Spaniards, Turks, and French sailors. It was intoxicatingly interesting.

How Jonah longed to go to Tarshish. He was sent to ministry in Nineveh instead. Nineveh was the known world. It was boring, stuck in its own long history. It was full of cantankerous and grumpy people, people who were all too aware that they weren't in Tarshish. Ministry in Nineveh wasn't often a lot of fun. But God sent Jonah there and made those people to be God's people.

It takes an act of courage and a daily dose of prayer to say that my own Nineveh, wherever it may be, is my home. It is always so tempting to imagine that everything would be different, better, more exciting somewhere else. And that all the people somewhere else would easily fit into my scheme of what the church should be. And that ministry would be smooth sailing and always fulfilling. It takes a continuously regenerated heart to know that the people I've already got are my people and I am their pastor. And that I am to pastor in this place, to this place, on behalf of this place.

"You can't know who you are until you know where you are," Wendell Berry said. And that knowing, and the serving that flows from it, is built from stability and fidelity. It points to the God who is rock, refuge, and strength. In a time of constant change, shallow roots, and ever-distracted attention, the work of ministry witnesses to the reliable, trustworthy, enduring presence of the Holy One who still and always lives in our and every neighborhood.

---

*And the bow shall be in the cloud; and I will look upon it, that I may remember the everlasting covenant between God and every living creature of all flesh that is upon the earth.*

—Genesis 9:16 (KJV)

# Paying It Forward

---

*God's kingdom is like yeast that a woman works into the dough for dozens of loaves of barley bread—and waits while the dough rises.*

—Matthew 13:33 (*THE MESSAGE*)

---

**P**ay it forward. That phrase became part of common parlance thanks to the 2000 Warner Bros. film called *Pay It Forward*. Starring Kevin Spacey, Helen Hunt, and Haley Joel Osment, it's about a young boy, Trevor McKinney, troubled by his mother's alcoholism and fears of his abusive but absent father. His new social studies teacher captures his imagination with an intriguing assignment—to think of something to change the world and then put the idea into action. Trevor comes up with the idea of paying a favor not back, but forward—repaying good deeds not with payback, but with new good deeds done to three new people. His efforts bring about something of a revolution not only in the lives of himself, his mother, and his physically and emotionally scarred teacher but also in those of an ever-widening circle of people completely unknown to him.

Pay it forward. For a long time, I have thought of a big part of my calling to ministry in terms of giving back and investing in others the same love and support that brought me to a place where I could hear God's call in my life and live into it. Others could see the spark in me before I could clearly see it myself. Others kept nudging me along when I was tempted to walk away. Others would call out my gifts when I doubted. Others opened doors for me to experiences of ministry in the larger church and in the world far beyond what I could ever have imagined on my own. I have a really strong sense that it's only right that I return the favor, the many acts of kindness and graciousness, as best I can.

I have mentored many candidates for ministry and new pastors over the years. Some days I think it's the very best part of what I do. God places the yeast just where it needs to be, but the process of baking bread requires someone to knead and wait and discern when the time is right. That's what a mentor is called to do. Sometimes mentors push back and help someone reflect. Sometimes mentors simply wait for the confidence to be strong and clear enough to take hold and rise. Mentors can point and prod. Mostly mentors walk alongside and teach through presence and by example. It's never easy to step aside and acknowledge a mismatch. I've been paired with folks for whom my style or my approach was not what was helpful, and we have parted ways amicably. I have been assigned to mentor folks who were so lackadaisical about the process that they could never even seem to get it together to simply show up on time for our meetings. I figured then that it was my job to help them see that ministry asks, indeed requires, much more of us than we are ever prepared to give.

Then there are the candidates for ministry whose experience of coming to terms with their call is not so much a walk as it is a wrestling match á la Jacob. It lasts a long night of the soul. And if in the morning, they limp a little, it is a sign of God's tenacious presence and an indication of a strength and tenacity that will serve them well over the long haul.

There's nothing more humbling than someone I've mentored saying, "I learned that from you." That's the thing about being a mentor that constantly keeps me fresh and self-reflective. Am I worthy of their trust? Is my ministry worthy of their emulation? Is God forming us into a company of faithful disciples who, together, will keep telling the story well enough to convince others of its very good news?

In the most wondrous of circumstances, the process of mentoring, paying it forward, culminates in ordination and the privilege, in our United Methodist tradition, of joining our bishop and other elders in "the laying on of hands." The yeast of the Holy Spirit has worked to bring forth new leaders for the church and the privilege of having a part in the process brings gratitude without measure.

---

*I'm reminded of your authentic faith, which first lived in your grandmother Lois and your mother Eunice. I'm sure that this faith is also inside you. Because of this, I'm reminding you to revive God's gift that is in you through the laying on of my hands. God didn't give us a spirit that is timid but one that is powerful, loving, and self-controlled.*

—2 Timothy 1:5-7 (CEB)

# Finding Funny

**M**inistry can be deadly serious work. I'm convinced that the only way not only to survive but to minister effectively is to find the humor in things that present themselves and laugh—at situations that arise, at encounters with people that take a detour, at ourselves.

A few years ago, we launched what has become an annual and much-beloved "Blessing of the Animals" service on or around Saint Francis's Day in early October. We've blessed cats, photos of cats too scared to venture from home, a snake, a lizard, desert tortoises, birds, a hamster, guinea pigs, a gerbil, a rat, photos of pets recently departed brought by still-grieving human companions, and lots of dogs. For the most part, these are rescue dogs whose social skills are still under development. It can get pretty chaotic, though most everyone calms down mysteriously for the prayers.

One year we were constrained to schedule a memorial service in the chapel adjacent to the courtyard at the time of the blessing of said animals. Assured that the deceased had been an animal lover, we thought this could all work out and had carefully scheduled the arrival of the hearse and the casket after the event should have been winding down. However, of course, this was the one day the mortuary folks arrived early. Nothing can match the memory of the attendant rushing around the rambunctious, newly blessed dogs to find me and proclaim loudly, "Pastor—the body is here! The body is here!"

Maybe we shouldn't be surprised, given our central narrative, that bodies—of the four-legged, two-legged, and even the slithery kind—factor in our most humorous moments. Life, death, and resurrection pretty much tell the whole story, after all.

The first Easter Sunday in my new church was traumatic. I was so nervous about the big crowd, the expectations of perfection, the performance aspect of it all, and the obvious fact that it was THE MOST IMPORTANT DAY OF THE YEAR. I could hardly breathe. I worked and reworked and reworked the sermon. Gallows humor was about the best I could manage going in: "If I live through this, I'll be fine!" which truly seemed to miss the point. The day arrived. The crowds materialized. The music was stupendous with brass, choir, tympani, and all-stops-out organ. The sermon was presentable, and the preacher didn't pass out. My cheeks ached from smiling as I greeted person after person at the narthex door. That's when it started. Comment after comment about how nice everything was "except for the lilies." "Too bad about the lilies." Down-turned eyes, painful looks. "If only for the lilies."

*What about the lilies?* I'm thinking to myself. They looked fine to me—rows and rows of them filled the chancel steps to overflowing. To each regretful comment, I had simply nodded seemingly knowingly, as if I concurred. Finally I couldn't bear it any longer. "What about the lilies?" I queried. "Well, they weren't *open!*" someone whispered conspiratorially. Ahhh . . .

I wanted to hear about the music, the sermon, the message of The Big Day! But no. It was all about the lilies. Gives whole new meaning to Jesus's direction to "consider the lilies" (Luke 12:27). Finally, in response to the umpteenth comment about the lilies, I said as straightforwardly as I could muster, "Well, you know, several choir members are allergic, so we arranged for the lilies to remain closed." You'd have thought I'd delivered the stone tablets! "Really? That's marvelous! Good for you!" I shamelessly took credit for the whole ridiculous thing. The staff and I laughed about it for months. Consider the lilies, indeed.

Sometimes when you want to cry or scream, you just have to laugh. You have to find funny in the midst of this wondrous life and God's never-to-be-taken-for-granted people. And since we're apparently created in God's image, each and every one of us, the very human quirks and foibles that bring tears of all kinds to our eyes show us something about the divine as well. I haven't quite figured all that is, except that I'm confident that there must be a lot of laughter in heaven. And God must surely have uttered an uproarious guffaw after rolling away that huge stone from the door of the tomb.

---

*All things bright and beautiful, all creatures great and small,*
*all things wise and wonderful: the Lord God made them all.*
*God gave us eyes to see them, and lips that we might tell*
*how great is God Almighty, who has made all things well.*

—Cecil Frances Alexander, "All Things Bright and Beautiful"

# The Soundtrack

*Music strikes in me a deep fit of devotion,*
*and a profound contemplation of the First Composer.*
*There is something in it of Divinity more than the ear discovers.*

—Thomas Browne

A friend visiting our worship service, himself an Episcopal priest, observed that the sermon had been based on a hymn. He'd never seen that done and mused that it must be something peculiarly Methodist. It seemed perfectly normal to me, daughter of the Wesleys as I am. Brother Charles knew that the music of the church would carry the preaching of the church straight to the heart, to the deeper reaches of faith and trust. My memory is filled up with verse upon verse of hymn after hymn, the ones we sang in church, the ones I learned in choirs, the ones my grandfather sang in the pickup truck as we drove along through the Arizonan desert where I grew up.

The psalmist proclaimed long ago that all peoples praise God with sounds and songs and rhythm. Tangos and tympani, bluegrass and Bach, psalms and sonatas, chorales and choruses, folk and fugue, bells and baritones—all to the glory of God, as Bach himself would have said. All our sounds and songs and rhythms give praise to our God.

We humans seem to be born with what Dr. Oliver Sacks calls "musicophilia," the love of music. He writes in his book by that name that "for virtually all of us, music has great power, whether or not we seek it out or think of ourselves as particularly 'musical.' This propensity to music—this 'musicophilia'—shows itself in infancy, is manifest and central in every culture, and probably goes back to the very beginnings of our species" (*Musicophilia: Tales of Music and the Brain* [New York: Random House, 2008], ix–x). Music occupies more areas of our brain than does language and lies deep in human nature.

## The Soundtrack

Every Sunday, a song calls our children up to the front of the sanctuary for the children's message. "This, this is where children belong, welcomed as part of the worshipping throng." The music signals welcome to the children who run forward eagerly. The words have helped establish a deep conviction in a once adult-focused setting that children are Christ's beloved disciples, too.

All who offer pastoral care learn that often the best way to connect with and comfort a beloved senior member who seems beyond speech or even recognition is to sing the hymns of the church. You might find that member moving his or her lips or even singing along. One longtime member would call the church frequently to complain that it was long past time for the pastor to bring her communion. Never mind that we celebrated it in worship once a month. She was on her own clock. Although her conversation rambled and repeated, she would mouth the words of the liturgy along with me, receive the elements, and then begin singing "In the Garden." We sang our duet visit after visit until her death and now I hear her still.

Music lies deep, deep within us. It has the power to soothe and heal. It has the power to restore memory. It has the power to connect us to God and to one another even through times when our hearts are broken or when God seems far away or when our ability to speak has gone.

Every Sunday, a retired pastor worships in a pew toward the front. His eyes are bright, though his ability to reason and speak is limited now to formalized greetings and pleasantries. But when the music starts, he raises his right hand and begins to conduct and sway gently. His arm rides the waves of rhythm, and a peace seems to come over him. Invariably he smiles, as if the hand of God has reached out to his, and in the music he hears, "You are my beloved."

---

*My life flows on in endless song, above earth's lamentation.*
*I hear the clear, though far-off hymn that hails a new creation.*
*No storm can shake my inmost calm while to that Rock I'm clinging.*
*Since love is Lord of heaven and earth, how can I keep from singing?*

. . . . . . . . . . . . . . . . . . . . . . . . . . . . . . . . . . . . . . . . . . . . . .

*The peace of Christ makes fresh my heart, a fountain ever springing!*
*All things are mine since I am his! How can I keep from singing?*

—Robert Lowry, "My Life Flows On
(How Can I Keep from Singing)"

CPSIA information can be obtained at www.ICGtesting.com
Printed in the USA
LVOW01s1433150815

450160LV00005B/6/P